GRAND FINISHES

For Walls and Floors

"A basic presentation of three home-improvement projects . . . in unintimidating plain talk. Instructions are friendly and offer a pointedly ecological awareness. . . . A good book for coaxing the wary beginner."

—*Publisher's Weekly*

M

GRAND FINISHES

For Walls and Floors

INTERIOR HOUSE PAINTING, WALLPAPERING, AND WOOD FLOOR REFINISHING

by Matt Nikitas

The
Globe
Pequot
Press

OLD SAYBROOK, CONNECTICUT

Diagram on page 9 based on illustration from *The Family Handyman* magazine, June 1993.
Cover and text design by Nancy Freeborn.
Illustrations by Matt Nikitas.
Photos by Don Seaver.

Library of Congress Cataloging-in-Publication Data

Nikitas, Matt.
   Grand finishes for walls and floors : interior house painting, wallpapering,
and wood floor refinishing / by Matt Nikitas. — 1st ed.
      p. cm.
   ISBN 1-56440-487-0
   1. House painting. 2. Paperhanging. 3. Wood finishing. 4. Flooring,
Wooden—Maintenance and repair. I. Title.
TT323.N55 1994
698'.14—dc20   94-31857
                                                      CIP

Manufactured in the United States of America
First Edition/Second Printing

This book is dedicated to
Alison Lazarus,
who is one of the grandest souls I know.

CONTENTS

REFINISHING WOOD FLOORS, 67

FINISHING TOUCHES, 87

ACKNOWLEDGMENTS

Special thanks to Hampton Coley, Ed Cameron, Teryl Tagg, Mike Nikitas and Amy Evans, Rich Howard, Don Graydon, Betty Greenwood, Brian Leahy, Kathy Nikitas, Don Seaver, Bill Melcher, Creative Paints of San Francisco, Mark Sidmore, Paul and Jose (everyone actually) at Toolmasters of San Francisco, Andy Tobias, John and Mary Nikitas, Ray Bodtmann, Jim and Henry from Wallstreet S.F., and Austin and Cleo Barrett (mom), and extra special thanks to Connie Burd of The Benjamin Moore Company and to Laura Strom.

INTRODUCTION

You are in the driver's seat. The information in this book will help you, but you are in control. Whether you are planning to paint your whole house or just one room, wallpaper a bathroom or living room, or refinish your floors, this book will provide all the instruction you need to do the job, and do it well. You should begin by having faith in yourself—your judgment and your ability.

You are the one who can judge when it is time to plan a home improvement project. Doing it yourself not only means being willing to do the work, but having the time and resources to accomplish the task you have in mind. The fact that you're reading this book is some indication that you've decided on a project. Congratulations! Making the decision is the first, and sometimes the biggest, step. Believe it or not, the rest can be fun, easy, and satisfying.

The bottom line for any kind of home improvement project is to trust your instincts. You know your own work style, and you know what you hope to accomplish. How to go about the work is something you can learn from this book, but it is your own good common sense that will take you through the job with flying colors.

1

HOW TO GET THE MOST OUT OF THIS BOOK

To familiarize yourself with the project you've chosen, why not settle back and read about it first? You'll find complete information in the book on each job, including step-by-step instructions for doing the work.

Then at the end of each main section, I've condensed that particular job into the specific steps to follow, along with the tools and materials needed.

GETTING A GOOD START ON A GRAND FINISH

So you're ready to get started on a project. First of all, there are some basics that apply to any home improvement job. I know; I make a living at it. So no matter what you're planning, the tips that follow are equally important for any job, big or small.

WRITE EVERYTHING DOWN

This is simple but important advice. A vital part of your planning for a project is to keep a record of the main points you want to remember and of the questions you want answered.

Before contacting stores for the tools and supplies you need, try jotting down pertinent information and questions as you go through the chapters in this book. Then you'll know exactly what products to ask for and how much of each to buy. You might use a yellow or fluorescent marker to highlight material you want to refer back to. And we've left some blank pages in the back of the book for your notes.

This planning will pay off when you get to the store. I tend to feel a little pity when I'm at a paint or hardware store ordering supplies, and I see an average guy (or gal) walk in—and it becomes obvious that this person's planning has begun right there in the store. The whole burden of information and preparation—not to mention trust—is placed entirely in the hands of the clerk.

Most salespeople enjoy providing information, but you should avoid relying solely on them. And they will probably appreciate your advance preparation, especially in a busy store. You just want to be sure you get enough information to feel comfortable.

LET YOUR FINGERS DO THE WALKING

Using the telephone first can save lots of time and trouble later. The expression "work hard, or work smart" is very appropriate to home improvement. Using the phone is working smart.

Did you ever notice that while you're waiting in a store to talk to a salesperson, maybe with one or two people in front of you, and everything stops when the phone rings? Whoever is calling gets his or her question answered while the clerk will ask you to hold on a minute. Consider this: The person on the other end of the line could be you!

Phone the paint and hardware supply stores first. Ask the questions you've jotted down. Ask them, for example: "Do you carry this product?" or "Do you know who might carry it?" This is a good time to get prices, too, so you can begin to figure out how much your job will cost you. After your telephone research turns up the best stores for you, go there in person. Of course, once you get to a store, you may think of new questions to ask. And when you get the answers you need, don't forget to write them down.

HAVE THE RIGHT TOOL FOR THE JOB

Over and over since my business was established, these words from my dad have echoed in my head: "Have the right tool for the job." If you need to plaster a large wall area, don't try doing it with a two-inch putty knife. Tasks attempted with the wrong tool will only frustrate you and make the job more difficult than it needs to be and take the enjoyment out of it. You'll find that a tool has been made for each job, and that with it your task will go much smoother.

Although you shouldn't plan to improvise when it comes to tools, you needn't be afraid to do what's necessary to get the job done either. You're ready to stir the paint, for example, but the dog has run off with your paint stirrer, and the paint store is closed. A wooden coat hanger might do just fine. If the choice is either to take a bit longer to stir your paint or to put off painting the room until the next day, well . . .

THE VOICE OF EXPERIENCE

Keep Pets in Their Place

Animals are wonderful, but most don't mix with home improvement jobs. Kittens and puppies will almost certainly inspect every move you make. As soon as a piece of newspaper goes down, both will find this a signal to come over and move it, immediately. They should probably be out in the yard, garage, or somewhere else when you're ready to work. Fully grown dogs are usually okay around a painting job, although those real friendly ones will undoubtedly wag their tails into a freshly painted wall. Adult cats, though more sedate than kittens, will wait until you've painted a certain door casing and then walk right over and give it a nice rub (you know, from the side of the mouth to the hind leg).

Should I Hire a Contractor?

Can you do the work? American do-it-yourselfers spend over $9 billion a year on home improvement supplies, so I think you can. If, however, you've got three kids, and you work a sixty-hour week while your husband works an eighty-hour week—well, maybe hiring help is the way to go. (Anyway, if you work a combined week of 140 hours, then have a heart, and give a contractor some work.)

If you decide to go with a professional, this book will help you in talking with contractors. You'll have a good idea of the work they're going to do, what to ask for, and what the heck those suggestions of theirs mean. When they start in with their contractors' lingo, you can either nod in understanding or know what questions to ask.

Try to get a work schedule from your contractor, and try to see that he or she sticks to it. For small jobs, our company asks for 50 percent of the cost of the job upon signing the contract and scheduling the work, with the balance due upon completion. If the job is over $3,000, we usually ask for 25 percent midway through the work, with the final 25 percent due on completion. For us, completion means when the client (that's you) is happy with the work and is satisfied that the contract has been fulfilled.

We are a capitalist society. We work; we get paid for the work. But be sure you are completely satisfied before you make that final payment. I think most contractors are interested in doing a good job—one that will make their client happy. But once a contractor has been paid in full, the job somehow registers as complete. I hate to admit it, but if a client paid us the final balance while there were still a few odds and ends left (we call this the "punch list"), we would have less incentive to come back to finish them. So go over the work with your contractor at the end of the job; as soon as the little touch-ups on your punch list are complete, pay the contractor in full, and you'll both be happy.

And beware of the temptation to play General Contractor! On jobs that involve two or more professionals—for example, a painter, a plumber, and an electrician—the general contractor is the person who hires everyone and brings it all together. The general contractor makes sure each job is done properly and at the right time in the correct order: that A happens before B, and that B is finished just before C is to begin.

I've gone into more jobs than I care to remember where the client (you) decided to save money by doing without a general contractor (whose bill typically will be the other contracted work totals plus 10 percent to 25 percent). If you need some plumbing, electrical work, and finish painting done, you may ask yourself: Why not just hire a plumber, an electrician, and a painter? But if the electrician comes back to finish running wire to a switch after the painting has been completed, who is going to patch the wall? Electricians will say it's not their job—and your painter may point out that the terms of the painting contract have been met. But a general contractor will take on the responsibility of such scheduling headaches, and all you have to do is take delivery of the finished job.

you know what they say about putting off until tomorrow. It's tough to anticipate absolutely everything, so you do need to be a little flexible.

FIND A HELPER

Tasks seem to become easier and more enjoyable with companionship. Your project will probably go better with a helper, and you can save a lot of time—especially if you are hanging wallpaper. Throughout a wallpapering job, you'll find yourself doing one thing while your helper handles another part of the work that needs to be done at the same time. You can hold up that sheet of wet, gluey wallpaper as your partner smooths it in place. Your helper might be a friend or a member of your family. (Remember Lucy and Ethel in that hilarious episode of "I Love Lucy"?)

Individual work styles are very different, so keep that in mind as you plan the job with the friend or family member who has agreed to help. Decide which tasks each of you will handle. If you have never worked before with your helper, ask what he or she would feel comfortable doing. If your helper becomes more ambitious during the project, great. In the meantime, keep your expectations realistic and make them clear to your partner. The last thing you need is to argue over who will do what or how it is to be done.

> ### THE VOICE OF EXPERIENCE
>
> ## A Friend in Need
>
> I recently helped a friend lay a new self-adhesive kitchen floor, and we both figured it would be a quick job. What we didn't anticipate was how long it would take to pull up the old floor (or the gooey tar that came up with the old tiles and seemed to leave itself on every surface in sight). We had both made plans for later in the day. As the afternoon drew to a close, so did our patience. The floor got finished, but not without bickering over the fastest method to use.

ESTIMATE HOW MUCH TIME YOU'LL NEED

How long is the job going to take you? You can drag it out as long as you want, or you can work around the clock and try to set a new world record.

The prep work is almost always the biggest chunk of the job. The time it takes to prepare surfaces for paint or wallpaper depends on you and on how meticulous you decide to be. For example, you may be able to breeze through the repair work in an hour, or take your time and use up the whole day.

And then getting the area ready (so that plaster, paint, and dust doesn't get everywhere) is another little part of the prep work that can't be overlooked. Moving furniture and laying down newspaper and drop cloths for two good-size rooms (perhaps 15 by 20 feet each) can probably be done in an hour or less if you've got a friend to help.

You and a friend should be able to paint the walls and ceiling in those two rooms in a few hours (less than half a day). The rest of the painting—involving, say, four doors, five windows, a base molding, and a set of bookshelves—could be finished up in another day. As for wallpapering that 4-by-5-foot bathroom, the one you've already taken an hour to prepare: You and a pal (a small one) might finish it with a couple of hours and a little sweat (I always sweat when I'm hanging wallpaper; that little bit of anxiety helps me do a really great job).

Enjoyment is the most important part of do-it-yourself renovating. If for you, that means taking your time, with lots of breaks, then great! Take this into account in planning your time. Or you might be a person who likes to speed through a job non-stop. Either way, you should be able to get an idea of the time you'll need by reading up on the job in this book and then factoring in your own work style.

THE VOICE OF EXPERIENCE

Some Beethoven and Pretzels Maybe?

How about a little music as a companion? I, myself, have almost always brought a radio or tape player to a jobsite, whether other workers were going to be there or not, and I've listened to a wide variety of things, from National Public Radio commentaries to Aerosmith's Greatest Hits. So many factors will determine what kind of music you'll choose to accompany you on your home improvement project—your age, where you live, who you live with, etc.

The one common thread, though, seems to be the motivation factor. What mood are you in today, and what will it take to get you going? It may be a really dramatic Italian opera, like Puccini's *La Boheme,* or it could be Mozart. My brother tells me he starts off his projects listening to The Who (which has always been his favorite rock band), but switches to classical once the caffeine from his coffee kicks in. His favorite is Beethoven's Pastoral, Symphony no. 6. Sometimes I feel that The Carpenters has just the perfect amount of light rock that I want. Other times, especially if I know I'll be alone all afternoon, motivation may come to me from self-reflection triggered by some New Age stuff that's not a downer, like George Winston.

Snacks are also a very personal thing. Having something around to munch on is an important part of my renovation work, and I have my own preferences, but I wanted some other opinions. So I asked many different people of all different ages what they snack on when taking on a project. Some say doughnuts, some say pastrami sandwiches (none said doughnuts *and* pastrami sandwiches). As with music, most people don't want a food that's going to slow them down. My sister pointed out that you probably wouldn't want to choose Cheetos because you run the risk of getting orange fingerprints on your newly painted walls. Remarkably, the one food that was mentioned by everyone I spoke with, and the thing I always choose first, is pretzels. They've got carbohydrates for energy, they're low in fat, and they're not messy. To wash them down, the general concensus seemed to be that a nice big diet soda or iced tea does the trick, probably because of the caffeine.

INTERIOR PAINTING

A h, to repaint your living space—what a rewarding experience! Ever since we humans have been setting up house, we've tried to beautify and personalize our surroundings, but it hasn't always been easy. Take the cavemen, for example. They painted pictures on their walls, a process that took a long time, no doubt, and, once completed, the pictures were there for an even longer time (tens of thousands of years, actually). It was the Egyptians who developed architectural coatings, around 2000 B.C., and figured out quicker ways to get them on the wall. They used brushes fashioned out of animal hair. In Colonial times milk derivatives were used to paint surfaces. Unfortunately, they tended to smell a bit sour when used indoors.

Today we've got all kinds of wonderful paint products for our homes, not to mention all the quick and easy ways to get them on the wall. With a little time and effort and not much money, we can bring in a new color just about anytime we want and give our home a fresh look—maybe even give ourselves a more positive outlook. It's great. I like to think of it as "the power of positive painting" (in fact, that's what I called my cable TV show). So read on. I'll tell you everything you need to know to do the job well.

THE PAINT ITSELF

Before we get to the how-to of painting, I want to run you through some basics about the paint itself. There are all different kinds of products out there that you can put on your walls and ceilings and floors.

THE CHEMISTRY OF PAINT

Paint has three principal components: solvent, binder, and pigment. Paint also includes a number of additives.

THE SOLVENT makes up the largest percentage of a paint and is the vehicle for the other ingredients. The solvent is also considered the drying agent. (States with the strictest environmental codes limit the solvents in non-latex paints, meaning the paint may take a bit longer to dry than it used to.) In latex

paint, water is the solvent; in alkyd products, it's mineral spirits (and other petroleum thinners).

THE BINDER contains the resins, which are what you're really paying for. A high quality and large amount of resin equals more expensive paint. In latex paint, the resins are the acrylics; in alkyds, they are the alkyd, epoxies, and oils (linseed, soybean, or tung).

THE PIGMENTS are the same in both latex and alkyd products. Titanium dioxide is a pigment that replaces the lead of yesteryear (and is the hiding agent). Titanium dioxide is expensive, and you'll find a good amount of it in a high-quality product. Other pigments are talc, clay, calcium carbonate, and zinc oxide (which replaces the mercury that used to be in paint).

THE ADDITIVES go into the paint along with all this other stuff. The additives include thickeners, fungicides, defoamers, driers, and surfactants. (These all do just what they sound like they might do: thicken, dry, etc.)

THE TYPES OF PAINT

Basically there are four types of paint: latex, alkyd, oil- and epoxy-based, and polyurethane.

LATEX PAINTS (generally known as water-based) have acrylics as resins. Latex paints are ideal for most walls and ceilings. They are easy to use, have a very low odor, and clean up with soap and water.

ALKYD PAINTS have alkyd as the main resin. When most of us think of oil-based paints, what we are really referring to are alkyd paints. Alkyd is a synthetic oil consisting of alcohol and acid. Alkyd paint has an odor while being applied. It requires mineral spirits (paint thinner) for cleanup. (A special note about alkyd paints: They contain volatile organic compounds, VOCs, which are released into the air as the paint dries, creating undesirable ground-level ozone. VOCs are one gauge by which environmentalists and lawmakers rate the level of pollution from a paint.)

OIL-BASED AND EPOXY-BASED PAINTS contain oil and epoxy resins. They're also unfriendly to the environment and to your lungs. They dry to an extremely hard and durable finish, however, and so are ideal for painting floors. Cleanup is with paint thinner.

POLYURETHANES contain plastic resins and are just that when dry: a clear plastic coating. Alkyd-based polyurethanes tend to have an amber color to them and are ideal for floors and tabletops. Cleanup

with these is mineral spirits. There are also water-based polyurethanes available today (usually called urethanes), which tend not to have the yellow (amber) tint to them, and cleanup is soap and water.

The big paint companies have big research and development budgets and are constantly trying to meet consumer and government demands for environmentally friendlier products. Generally speaking, alkyd-based and oil-based products tend to be more durable than their latex counterparts. But you can now get alkyd-based paints with acrylic resins (normally associated only with latex paint). Odor-free and requiring only soap and water for cleanup, these new products bring us closer to having extremely durable paint without adding to air pollution. I hope we'll eventually replace the alkyd and oil-based products completely, which would be an important step toward respecting our planet a little more.

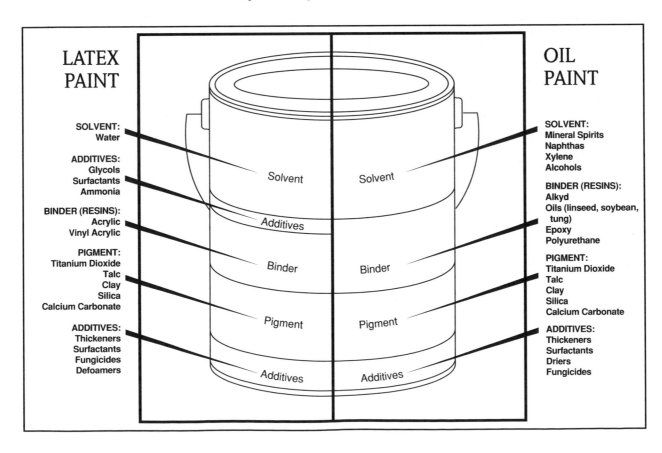

CHOOSING COLORS

You may have an idea what colors you'd like to use. But at this point, the colors may exist only in your head. It's now time to find an actual paint that matches the colors in your mind.

Paint manufacturers provide paint and hardware stores with their own swatch selections. These swatches, or chips, represent the colors they offer. Most swatches show custom colors, which the store can mix for you. The paint companies also provide the store with charts of premix colors; that is, paints in popular colors that are kept in stock and don't require any custom mixing and are generally less expensive.

You'll make things easier on yourself by sticking with the brand of paint whose swatches you've chosen. Each company may offer hundreds of its own color selections, but it's surprisingly difficult to match colors exactly from one brand to another.

Take some of these swatches home, and play around with them. Stick them on the wall, maybe near curtains or by a sofa that you're keen on working into the scheme. And definitely put the swatches in a place where you can see how they look in sunlight; it's amazing how colors change appearance from lamplight to natural light.

Some paint manufacturers have invested in computer equipment that can match colors exactly. Check with your paint store to see if they have the equipment and what they charge for the service. You can run to the store with a piece of fabric from your couch or your carpeting (or even with a chip off the wall of that restaurant that is painted just the color you're looking for). The computer system will look at these specimens and come up with the recipe to create the color you seek. Be warned though: Unless your sample is a completely true representation of the color (not glossy, dirty, or two-tone), the machine may not come up with the color you think you're seeing in the piece of fabric or chip.

I'm trying to stay away from blatant color suggestions that reflect my own personal taste. But at the same time, I've seen a lot of rooms, before and after painting, and it may help you to know what approaches to color have worked well. You might call these "standard" approaches, but they needn't be viewed as ordinary or boring or "what everyone else does." They are really what seems to work for a great many people.

With your choice of colors, you'll be making a personal statement, though I tend to think of it as basically a mood statement. The main statement of a room is made by its furniture, pictures, and other contents. The ceiling isn't usually the best place to make a bold color statement. It might be fun to paint the ceiling dark—but white, in a flat finish, is almost certainly the way to go. A tone of white is also the attractive, clean, and simple way to finish base moldings, crown moldings, doors, and window frames.

THE VOICE OF EXPERIENCE

The Many Colors of White

The term "white" turns out to be pretty relative. One large paint company sells a Navaho White, Linen White, Atrium White, and Off White—all variations of white, but some with a bit of creaminess, others with a little gray. The company's version of a true white, with no tinting whatsoever, is called Decorator's White. But I have used their Super White, which I honestly think is so close that I'd say they're both the same: white. Study each manufacturer's paint chips, and maybe you'll be able to figure out for yourself which white is white, and which one you'd like to see on your walls.

This leaves the walls as the place to make a color statement, your personal statement. I like pastels (light colors), but I also like rich, dark colors. Go with your own feelings. The decision isn't irreversible if it turns out to be a horrible choice. But gut instinct is usually the best indicator of what will look good to you. We just painted our living room walls a rich, dark green, leaving the ceiling and trim white. Of course, a darker wall color will tend to enclose a room and make it appear smaller. But it also can make a room cozier, depending upon your furniture and other surroundings.

Color experts have found that yellow is the most difficult color for the eye to process, thereby making hallways or transition rooms a good place for yellows. Reds apparently stimulate appetite (dining rooms), and blues and greens are the easiest on the eye, thereby being very soothing and restful (great for dens, living rooms, and children's rooms).

It's a good idea to "box" custom paint, that is, mix together all the gallons you have of one color. This ensures that any pigment variations from one gallon to the next will be eliminated. You can do it by either pouring all the cans of paint into a clean 5-gallon container or by pouring a little out of one can and then a little from each of the others into this gallon, and back and forth.

THE FINISH ON THE PAINT

Paints come in a progression of finishes, from flat to high gloss. Following is a quick look at the characteristics of each.

A **FLAT (OR MATTE) FINISH** does not reflect light because it has no sheen. A flat finish generally is used on ceilings and walls. This finish is not very scrubbable because of its porousness.

An **EGGSHELL FINISH** has a slight sheen and reflects light a bit. It works nicely on walls, and is washable and scrubbable.

A **SATIN FINISH** has a higher sheen than an eggshell finish. It works well on any wall where you're seeking light reflection. It also works well on trim and on bathroom and kitchen walls if you want a subtler look than you get with the more traditional semi-gloss finish in these areas. A satin finish won't absorb dirt, so it's very washable and very scrubbable.

A **SEMI-GLOSS FINISH** is traditionally used for trim, woodwork, and bathroom and kitchen walls—any areas that will see a good amount of traffic. Highly washable/scrubbable.

A **GLOSS FINISH** is also good for trim. It has a higher sheen than a semi-gloss. Highly washable/scrubbable.

A **HIGH-GLOSS FINISH** is just what it says—even shinier than a gloss finish. It provides the greatest reflection of light. On a smooth surface, it can look like glass. Highly washable/scrubbable.

THE VOICE OF EXPERIENCE

A Waste of Money

I don't like to rain on anybody's parade, but there are lots of products out there that are, well, frankly, a waste of money. For instance, I just came across a "latex paint conditioner" that is supposed to, when added to your paint, slow the drying time so that the brush marks will level out on your surface.

A friend of mine who is the West Coast coatings representative for the largest paint company in America says, "Garbage! A complete waste. If the product needed it, it would already be included. Otherwise it's just displacing necessary ingredients."

HOW MUCH PAINT WILL I NEED?

Paint makers usually estimate that a gallon of paint will cover somewhere between 350 and 400 square feet. That's normally an estimate for covering a flat finish (which absorbs a lot of paint). Because a fresh coat of paint is far less porous than an old one, you'll find that a second coat will require less paint than the first. And if you're painting over a glossy finish, the paint will go much further because the surface is not porous at all.

Almost always, you can plan on two coats. This is the safest bet for covering the old surface completely so that you'll be able to enjoy the new color with

none of the old color bleeding through. There's an exception to this two-coat rule: If your new color is darker than the paint now on the walls, one coat may cover just fine (especially if the old coat was applied within the past year). One other point: If you're paint-

ing over a very dark color, new wood, or a repaired area, you will first need to apply a coat of primer (see the section on priming later in this chapter).

Let's look at an average-size living room, one measuring 15 by 20 feet, with 8-foot-high walls and a couple of windows and doors. One gallon of paint should be enough for two coats on the ceiling. For the walls, one gallon should be enough for one coat; plan on using a second gallon if you want two coats. One gallon will be more than enough for the trim (the windows, doors, and molding).

Finally, a word of advice about the paint you buy: Use a high-quality name brand. You'll save money in the long run. Good paints cover much better, are easier to keep clean, and will probably last longer (thus extending the amount of time between paint jobs). And they can be a lot easier to apply because cheap paint tends to spray all over the place as you roll it on.

PREPARATIONS FOR PAINTING

Before you even open a can of paint, get the area ready. Let's look at what the room might need, so that once the painting begins, you and the surfaces and the surroundings (chairs, pictures!) will be ready.

TOOLS AND MATERIALS

You're going to need paint, OK. And getting ready for a paint job means gathering together a collection of tools and materials. The prep work comes first. The following list outlines some things you will want to have for repair work and other preparation duties.

PUTTY KNIFE: This indispensable tool is also called a blade or scraper or, if it's over 6 inches wide, a tape knife. The blade may be rigid or flexible.

JOINT COMPOUND: The compound usually comes in mixed (wet) form, making it easy to work with. It normally takes a few hours to dry. Other forms of joint repair material include gypsum, plaster, plaster of paris, drywall compound, and Spackle. Plaster usually comes in powder form, which is mixed with water. You'll find that pre-mixed joint compound is the easiest to work with (and mixing the joint compound with a little dry plaster will speed up the compound's drying time).

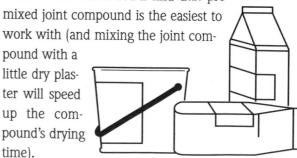

DRYWALL TAPE: The tape, also called joint tape, comes in rolls of either paper or cloth mesh, usually about 2 inches wide. The tape is usually applied with wet plaster (joint compound) to cover the gap between two new sheets of drywall. You can use small lengths of this tape to repair bad cracks or holes in walls.

DRYWALL: Also called Sheetrock, drywall consists of dried plaster held between two sheets of paper. It's usually used in new construction to make walls and ceilings, but small pieces are perfect for repairing holes in the walls or ceiling. Drywall is usually sold in 4-by-8-foot sheets and is available in various thicknesses from a quarter-inch to three-quarters of an inch. It can be cut very easily with a razor blade.

KEYHOLE SAW: This small, pointed saw is ideal for cutting small openings in pieces of drywall. (A steak knife also works fine, believe it or not!)

CAULK: There are many kinds available, but basic latex paintable caulk is easy to work with and can be painted once it dries. Cut off the very tip of the tube of caulk with a razor blade or scissors; then break the seal inside the plastic cone by shoving a nail into the opening.

CAULKING GUN: The gun works by putting pressure on the base of the tube of caulk, which is held in the gun. As you pull

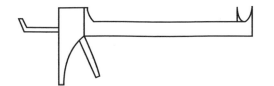

the trigger, caulk is forced out the tip of the tube. To stop the flow, push the tab located at the top of the handle (you'll hear it snap).

PAINT REMOVER: Here's a great chemical (if there is such a thing). It will lift the paint right off most surfaces. Definitely wear rubber gloves, and apply the remover with a pure bristle brush. Read the directions.

WALLPAPER REMOVER: This material is usually sold in a concentrate that you mix with water. It can be applied to wallpaper surfaces with a sponge or spray bottle.

WIRE BRUSH: You'll use this brush to help clean crumbling paint from crevices, edges of moldings, and window frames. Wire brushes come in all shapes and sizes (just like hairbrushes).

SANDPAPER: Keep a few sheets of this stuff handy— in fine, medium, and coarse grits—for the little sanding jobs that are always part of getting ready for painting.

SCREWDRIVERS: Both regular and Phillips-head screwdrivers are useful for such jobs as removing electrical switch and outlet plates, taking off door hardware, and opening paint cans.

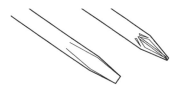

STEPLADDER: A 4-foot or 5-foot wooden or aluminum ladder will get you through almost any interior painting job. For low ceilings, a 2-foot ladder can be handy, and is easy to carry around.

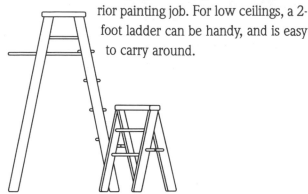

PREPARATIONS, STEP BY STEP

STEP 1: *Clear the Area*

Before you get too far into the project, you might as well figure on protecting the furniture and floors from damage. I mean, it may as well be done sooner rather than later.

Start by moving the furniture out of the way. Move as much as you can out of the room (less furniture to trip over and less furniture to have to cover). Move the remaining furniture at least three feet from any wall. This will leave you plenty of elbow, leg, and ladder room.

Put the furniture in manageable clumps; that is, avoid putting all the furniture in one pile in the center of the room where it would interfere with reaching part of the ceiling with your roller. Group the stuff into two or even three groups that are small enough to let you easily reach from one side to the other. Leave enough room between each group for you to walk (and again, think of ladder space). Throw a plastic drop cloth over each group of furniture.

To protect the floor, I use either a canvas drop cloth, moving it around as I go (careful to keep the same walked-on side up all the time), or newspaper. If you use newspaper, keep an eye on it. As you walk

on it, it tends to move; a bit of breeze will blow it around. The ink in many newspapers rubs off very easily, so I usually avoid using newspaper on carpeted floors.

The main point is to remember that whatever you don't cover will probably get sprayed or splattered during the preparation period and during the painting itself. It usually works out well to use a combination of drop cloths (canvas and plastic, and maybe an old sheet or two), along with some newspaper, for making sure you've covered everything that would look better without bits of joint compound or paint on it.

Before starting work around your place, lay out newspapers and dropcloths to cover any surfaces you'd prefer to keep clean.

At some point before you paint, you'll want to deal with any light fixtures, switch and outlet plates, and doorknobs. This really can be put off until just before the paint can is opened. A ceiling light fixture should have a cover plate that unscrews, enabling you to paint the ceiling under it. Then simply put the cover plate back in place when the painting up there is done.

Remove any switch and outlet plates with a screwdriver. Stick them in an envelope until you're done painting. Screw each little screw back into the

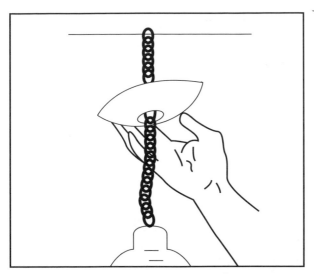

You can unscrew and move the ceiling plate on most light fixtures, enabling you to roll the paint around it easily.

hole it came from, without the plate (they have a habit of disappearing!). If the switch or outlet plates are old or have been painted over in the past, now would be a great time to throw them out and buy new ones. They don't cost much. (See page 97.)

STEP 2: *Remove Old Wallpaper*

Is there wallpaper on any of the surfaces you plan to paint? If so, it should probably come off. You can take a chance and paint over it, especially if you're only painting a small room off the basement. But I wouldn't. Because after some paint job—perhaps the one you're about to undertake—the old paper will probably buckle, or even come off in sheets. Yuck.

If you're lucky, the wallpaper will be strippable vinyl. Just grab a little corner, and peel the wallpaper off, strip by strip. Once it's off, chances are there will be a glue residue on the wall (maybe even some paper residue, if the vinyl was paper-backed). Put a drop cloth down to protect the floor; a wallpaper remover will get rid of the glue.

Follow the directions with the wallpaper remover and you'll be fine. Most require that you mix them with warm water and apply with a spray bottle or sponge. Cover about a 4-foot square of wall at a time. Let it sit for the specified time, then scrape the wet residue off with a broad-bladed (6 inches or so) putty knife. You'll get the hang of it. Try to be careful not to damage the walls.

What if the wallpaper is not strippable (in other words, you keep trying to lift off the covering at a flap but all you can get off is a shaving)? You can still get it off with the wallpaper remover. Take a sharp putty knife and score the walls, cutting through the coating on the face of the wallpaper with diagonal lines, creating diamond shapes that measure 1 or 2 inches across. Then apply the wallpaper remover.

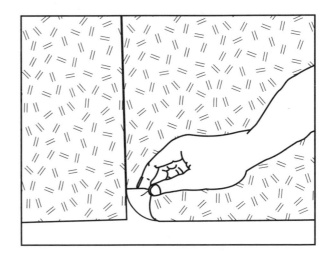

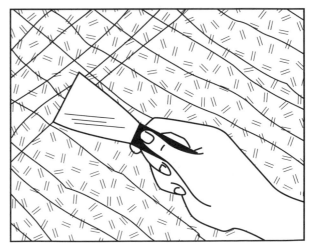

Is it strippable vinyl (above) *Grasp a corner and try to peel it off. If it won't come off easily, then you may have to score the walls* (below) *before applying wallpaper remover.*

This scoring is done to allow the remover to penetrate the paper and help lift it off the wall. Again, try to be careful not to damage the walls as you scrape off the paper. But don't freak out if you do; I make this mistake all the time. (Just see the information on wall repairs later in this section.)

You have one more option for removing wallpaper. You can try renting an electric wallpaper steamer to speed up removal of the paper and to help minimize damage to the wall. Check the stores in your area to see if a steamer is available for rent. I myself don't use them very often because I've had good luck with manual removal. But if you decide to try a steamer, just follow the directions; its use is pretty straightforward. But don't expect to get out of removing the glue that's left on the wall. Even with the steamer, you'll still end up having to remove the glue residue.

STEP 3: *Remove Paint Buildup and Loose Paint*

Door won't close? Window stick like crazy? Maybe the problem is paint buildup—too much paint around the edges or in the door jamb or window frame. It probably would be a good idea to get rid of some of this paint buildup before adding more.

There are a few ways I'd suggest for attacking paint buildup. First try and scrape the edges with

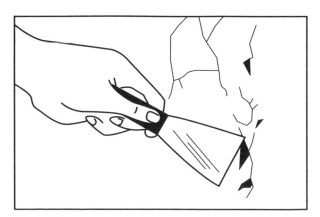

Scrape off any loose or peeling paint with your putty knife.

your putty knife, following up with sandpaper if you think the edges are still a little rough. You can also try paint remover. As mentioned earlier, if you use paint remover, wear rubber gloves, and apply the remover with a pure bristle brush. Follow directions on the can, and give edges a final sanding, just to clean up the jamb or frame.

I should mention that my suggestion to get rid of paint buildup is just that: a suggestion. Don't get crazy with this aspect of the job. Wood contains water, which slowly evaporates as the wood ages and may be absorbed when it's humid. Your doors and windows may continue to stick, paint buildup or not. So use your judgment.

Loose paint is another matter. If you spot cracks in the paint on your walls or find places where paint

THE VOICE OF EXPERIENCE

Scraping the Walls

There's no need to go hog wild with scraping walls in preparation for repainting. The key is to have a sound surface to paint on, without pulling down the lath, plaster, and studs. We were involved in many an old apartment in Manhattan where the prep work seemed endless, due to the age of the home, the severe winters, and previous lousy paint jobs. Depending on how far the client wanted to go to restore the place, I'd tell my guys to scrape as thoroughly as possible without an unreasonable amount of strength or elbow grease involved.

If you're tearing away at those wall surfaces with a vengeance, and it seems that the next step is to break out the jackhammer, chances are you're probably giving them a little more attention than they really need. It's all up to you and the amount of effort you'd like to give. Bear in mind that you can, and probably will, do wonders for the room with whatever prep work you can give it.

is flaking up or hanging off, you should do a little scraping to get the surfaces sound and clear, ready for paint. Your scraper will do the trick. Find what sections need attention, and scrape them from all angles. This should knock off all the loose fragments. Follow this up with a bit of wire-brush action. But it's not necessary to go overboard on this part of the project, either. If paint is separated from the wall or ceiling surfaces, then it should be scraped off. Just remember that whatever prep work you can give your surface will make a big difference.

STEP 4: *Repair Cracks, Holes, and Uneven Surfaces*

A variety of products are available to repair cracks and holes and areas where the paint has been scraped off. The products have a lot of different names that mean pretty much the same thing (though they may be slightly different in chemical makeup): joint compound, Spackle, plaster, wall-board compound, drywall compound, gypsum. For consistency, I'll use the word "plaster" in this section, but remember that this is just shorthand for any of these products that you choose to use. The plaster is a substance that, with the consistency of thick batter, is applied to cracks and holes in a surface. When it hardens, it will fill these irregularities, and you will (hopefully) be left with a completely flat surface.

In applying plaster over a bad spot in the wall, work with two putty knives: one with a blade that is 3 inches or so wide, and one with a blade at least 6 inches wide. Even better for this second tool would be a tape knife with a blade 10 inches wide. (If you are confident enough to work with a wider knife, say 12 inches or so, then great!)

Avoid putting too much plaster on your knife at a time. Use the wider blade on the wall surface to spread a nice thin layer over the area you're giving attention to. This part of the job can truly be con-

For uneven surfaces, apply plaster with a putty knife that's at least 6 inches wide (12-inch blade shown here).

sidered an art form, difficult to get the hang of. A professional plasterer commands good money. But you can do it too.

The trick (and there really is only this one trick) is to keep the wider blade clean each time it comes back in contact with the wall. Wipe plaster smoothly onto the wall with the wide blade, then scrape the excess plaster off its edge with the smaller knife; then once again smooth plaster on the wall with the wide blade, and again scrape the excess off with the smaller knife. It seems that the problems and frustrations come in when you don't wipe off the wide blade, and instead try to smooth new plaster on the wall with leftover plaster on the blade. Anyway, if some of the plaster on the wall ends up looking kind of lumpy, don't worry. Do the best you can, and let it dry. You can always put another bit on there, once dry.

17

Place the drywall tape over the crack, into the bed of plaster that you've laid.

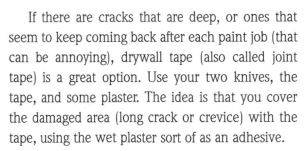

Work with a large and a small putty knife, wiping the larger one off each time before swiping the wall again with it.

If there are cracks that are deep, or ones that seem to keep coming back after each paint job (that can be annoying), drywall tape (also called joint tape) is a great option. Use your two knives, the tape, and some plaster. The idea is that you cover the damaged area (long crack or crevice) with the tape, using the wet plaster sort of as an adhesive.

Cut the tape with scissors to whatever length you need. Then spread some plaster with the smaller knife over the crack, being generous and putting it on a much wider area than the tape will cover. Place the piece of tape on the wet plaster that is covering the crack. Every portion of the tape should be sitting in wet plaster. Smooth the tape down by holding one end with the small knife as you pull the wide blade across the tape, forcing excess plaster out from under the tape. There should be no bubbles under the tape. When you finish pulling the wide blade across the tape, your repair patch is in place.

Hold one end of the tape with your finger and smooth it down by lightly draging your knife over the tape.

Let it dry, then give it a second coat with the wide knife. Eyeball all your other areas that have got first coats, and if they need another touch, go for it. This time around you pull a lot less plaster across your patched areas, so it should be a thinner coat (and easier to apply, too). By the way, this is called a skim coat. You also may have to do one more quick coat; check to see if the tape still shows through.

If the patch looks good to you after it has dried, go ahead and give it a light sanding. You can even wet-sand it with a sponge; that is, use a wet sponge instead of sandpaper. The plaster, being water soluble, will get smoother as you wipe it down, without creating any dust.

If there are crevices where a door molding meets the wall or between window and molding, it may be easier to repair with the caulk in the caulking gun rather than using plaster. Simply shoot the caulk into the cavity you'd like to close up, then smooth it with a wet finger.

If it's a very wide or deep crack, your caulk may just continue dropping in instead of filling it over (in other words, it could take tubes and tubes to fill the crack). Shove some newspaper into the crack to fill up the biggest part of the space. Then shoot in the caulking. To finish off the job smoothly, take a wet sponge (or even your dampened finger) and smooth

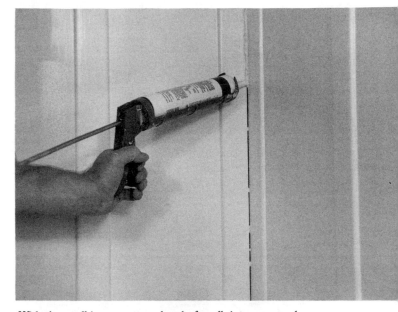

With the caulking gun run a bead of caulk into any cracks or crevices that you think might bother you later.

Smooth the bead of caulk in with a wet finger.

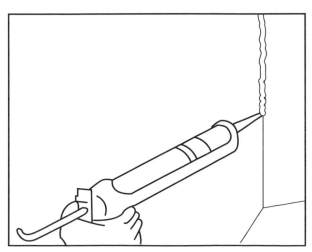

Caulk does wonders for cracks in corners.

the caulk. Since the caulk we're using is latex-based, which is water-soluble, it will conform nicely to the shape you give it.

Smooth the bead of caulk in with a wet sponge, thus wiping out the excess and doubly ensuring a complete seal.

THE VOICE OF EXPERIENCE

Read All About It

While working on the outside doorway of an old warehouse building on the lower East Side of Manhattan, we were scraping around the entry door's cement molding. It was crumbly and obviously hadn't been worked on for a long time. Beneath some petrified caulking, we pulled out some bunched-up newspaper that had been wadded into the crevices as a filler and as a base for the caulk. It was a New Jersey newspaper from 1902! After that I've always respected a worker's decision to use newspapers in this way.

You can also use wads of newspaper to fill in small holes in the wall. If the hole is tiny, you can just stuff a bit of paper in—so that it's wedged but not protruding—and plaster right over it, using the small putty knife. If the hole is a bit bigger—say, an inch and a half in diameter—again stuff paper inside and plaster over it. But then come back and strengthen the repair by covering it with joint tape, applying it the same way you would in repairing a crack. Again, once it's dry, skim another coat over it, then one more coat if it needs it.

STEP 5: *Repair the Larger Holes*

If the hole is bigger than that, a little artistry and ingenuity is called for. You'll need some plaster compound, your putty knives, a keyhole saw, a single-edge razor blade, and a small piece of drywall (a little bigger than the size of the hole). This kind of repair doesn't come up too often, so if you don't have a keyhole saw, an old steak knife will do fine.

With the keyhole saw, try to cut straight sides for the hole. This will merely make it easier for you to cut a matching piece of drywall to fit into the hole.

Drywall can be cut very easily. Drywall is really only a solid plaster sandwich, with paper as the bread. To cut it, start by running your razor blade through the paper on one side. Then tap the piece of drywall on the edge of a counter (or over your knee) on the other side of the drywall from where you have made the cut. This will break the drywall evenly on that line—but will still leave the paper attached on the other side. Now with the drywall in bent position, it's easy to slice the paper through on the other side, and, voila!, you have a clean separation.

The desired end result in preparing a drywall patch like this is to have a piece of drywall that fits nicely into the hole—but that also has some extra paper facing out that can lap over onto the wall and serve as a kind of drywall tape.

First cut yourself a piece of drywall that is an inch or so wider each way than the hole you are patching. (For example, if the hole measures 3 inches by 3 inches, cut a piece of drywall 5 inches by 5 inches.) Mark the actual dimensions of the hole onto this piece of drywall, centering them so that there's about an inch left along each side of the drywall.

Cut the paper along your marks, one edge at a time, but only on one side. After each cut, tap the drywall on the edge of a counter to break it on your line. Peel away the 1-inch-wide strip of drywall, but be careful not to tear off the extra flap of paper on the other side.

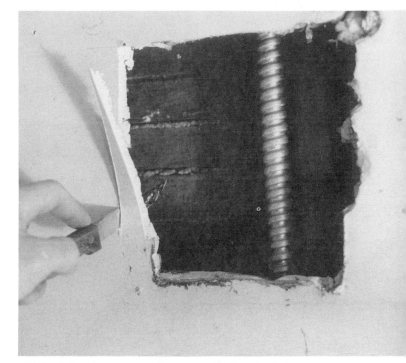

Cut the hole a bit squarer with a razor blade or keyhole saw (or steak knife).

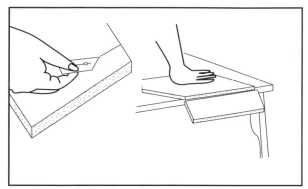

Use a single-edge razor blade to score the front of the drywall piece where you want to make a cut. Then lightly tap it (it'll easily break).

You should end up with a piece of drywall the size of the hole, but with an extra margin of paper on its face. Butter some plaster generously around the edges of the hole, then place your new patch into it, with the excess paper sitting over the edges of the hole and onto the wet plaster on the wall. Pull your putty knife along this extra paper in order to smooth out any excess plaster, and you'll have a super repair job! When it dries, give it another coat or two, the same as if it were joint tape. And lastly, sand.

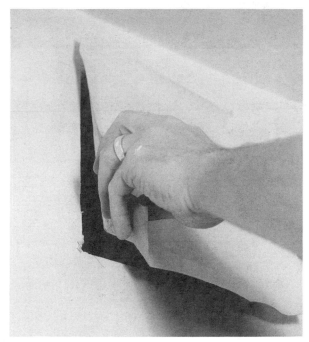

This will enable you to fit in your repair piece; make additional cuts in the hole if necessary.

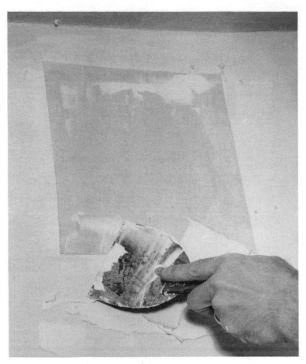

Plaster the edge of the hole under the patch paper flap (like you would with drywall tape) and then around the edge of the patch.

THE VOICE OF EXPERIENCE

Cutting Drywall Down to Size

Even with all the repair work I've done, I rarely buy sheets of drywall. It's not that it's expensive (maybe $8.00 a sheet). The problem is that drywall (also called Sheetrock or gypsum board) is manufactured and sold almost exclusively in 4-by-8-foot sheets—a cumbersome size to carry home from the store.

Instead of having to deal with a full sheet of the stuff for your modest projects, there are a few ways to go in order to get smaller pieces. We keep leftover pieces from earlier jobs. A lot of do-it-yourselfers have a similar stock of leftover pieces. Know anyone who fits that description? Ask them for a spare piece. Or if there's some new construction in your area, just ask one of the workers for a piece (I mean, all you

need is a small piece, and they would have tossed it out anyway).

Some stores are even beginning to sell half-sheets of drywall. And if worst comes to worst, you can go to a place that sells full sheets, buy a sheet, and cut it at the store into a half or quarters, thus enabling you to get it into your car.

STEP 6: *Start Clean*

It's written on the back of every can of paint that you'll come across: "All surfaces should be free of dirt, oil, grease, or peeling paint. Glossy surfaces should be dulled." We've pretty much taken care of the peeling paint. Usually the only additional thing to do is to dust the walls or molding.

Sometimes though, especially if we're talking about kitchens or bathrooms, there will be grease or mildew, stuff that will keep the fresh coat of paint from adhering properly. There is a product called TSP (which stands for trisodium phosphate). It's a cleaning solution that, when mixed with water, is ideal for getting surfaces free of all those things. Most housepainters use this.

And lastly, if any of the surfaces have a gloss to them, they should be dulled a little before repainting. This is called giving a tooth to the old finish, and you do it by merely running over the surface with sandpaper (using a minimal amount of effort).

PRIMING AND PAINTING

We still haven't opened the paint. The prep work's been completed, and now you may need to prime your area to make the surfaces ready for paint.

TOOLS AND MATERIALS

During the priming and painting, you'll need an expanded selection of items, in addition to primer and the paint itself.

PAINTBRUSH (PURE BRISTLE): A pure bristle brush made from horsehair or other natural fiber is perfect for oil-based and alkyd-based paints because it keeps its shape well. But this brush doesn't react well to water products. The bristles, when exposed to latex (water-based) paints, tend to expand and curl.

PAINTBRUSH (TYNEX OR POLYESTER): Use this one for latex paints. A good-quality paintbrush, when tapped or pulled, will not lose bristles. A close-up look should reveal bristles that are mainly of one length, but with a few flagged ends of varying lengths to ensure that the brush will hold paint and not drip. Your job will go much smoother, literally, with a good-quality brush. Cheap brushes lose bristles in the paint, and they hold less paint, which makes the job take much longer!

PAINT TRAY AND LINER: The liners are flexible, inexpensive, and disposable, and sit right in the tray itself, being the same shape. Use one for each color.

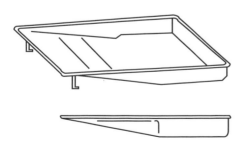

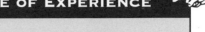

THE VOICE OF EXPERIENCE

Painting the Town

I absolutely adhere to the idea that home improvement projects should be enjoyable. But be careful about your thoughts of having a "painting party."

A client called me in to paint his kitchen and bedroom. "And, oh," he added, "could you do something about the paint on the floors? And maybe make the lines a little straighter here, where the moldings meet the wall?"

The place was really a mess, with paint all over the floor. The trim paint seemed to be on the trim, and on everything else as well. He had had a painting party, he told me. Seven of his friends had come by, and they had a great time painting his new apartment. He supplied all the materials, snacks, and, oh yeah, he served the beer.

I spent nine hours on the floors alone, trying to scrape and clean the hardwood floors without taking the finish off and then buffing and touching up as best I could.

So, have a painting party if you wish. But realize that while a group of friends may get the work done more quickly than one or two people would, the quality will suffer. You can't expect much individual responsibility or pride with lots of people doing the work (people who, I might add, won't be living there). And if you serve alcohol, kiss goodbye to any possibility of a good job.

ROLLER HANDLE: The roller handle is also known as a sleeve holder or paint handle.

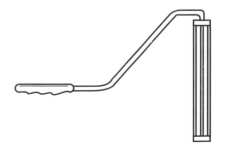

SLEEVE: The sleeve, which actually applies the paint, is also known as a roller. The sleeves come in various nap sizes (thicknesses). Generally, the smoother the surface you're painting, the shorter the nap you want to use. As with brushes, a natural fiber (mohair, for instance) is recommended for oil- and alkyd-based paints, whereas a synthetic fiber (like Dynel or polyester) is better for latex.

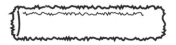

RAGS: Any old pieces of clothing will work great, but cotton is the best because it's so absorbent (which works best if you drip paint). An old pair of men's BVDs is perfect (hopefully they're clean), or a T-shirt (cut off the sleeves and cut the middle section into pieces).

DROP CLOTHS: They come in lots of sizes, in canvas or plastic. A 9-by-12-foot canvas drop cloth is a manageable size and is a good investment (about $25) if you're planning to paint several rooms. Plastic drop cloths are cheaper and great for draping over your furniture for protection. Again, 9 by 12 is a handy size, but you can also get them much larger. You can easily cut the plastic into smaller sizes. Plastic drop cloths come in varying thicknesses, called mils (a mil is a thousandth of an inch). A thickness of 1 mil to 2 mils is fine. And don't forget your old worn-out sheets; they also are perfect as drop cloths (if they don't have too many holes).

CLEANUP SUPPLIES: For cleanup of oil- and alkyd-based paints, you'll need mineral spirits (paint thinner). Latex paints require only soap and warm water. A supply of single-edge razor blades is good for cleaning paint off the glass on windows.

A PRIMER PRIMER

Primer generally comes in white and serves two purposes:

- It creates a "clean slate" for the paint, allowing the new paint to show its true color, with no chance of the old color showing through.

- It neutralizes "hot spots"—like a plaster patch, a moisture stain, or new wood—creating a sound surface for the paint to bond to. (If you paint directly over new plaster, with no primer coat, you can expect hairline cracks to begin appearing within a month.)

Ideally, the best way to go is to apply a full coat of primer followed by two coats of paint. Invest in a top-quality latex primer, because cheapie primer often requires two applications to cover darker colors. Most primers need to dry for just a few hours before application of the paint; some require even less time. Double-check the label of your primer.

I've had many clients who wanted to save a little money and so just had us do "spot priming." Yes, as you guessed, spot priming means to skip the full prime coat and to just prime over any hot spots, like plaster patches or new wood. If you spot-prime with a high quality primer and follow up with two coats of finish paint, you'll probably cover the old color on the walls just fine—unless the walls were previously a dark color, darker than the new paint.

PAINTING, STEP BY STEP

There are two ways to get paint on the surfaces: roller and brush. (There is spraying, too, but that's another ball game.) Use the brush for areas you can't get at cleanly with the roller, like corners, edges, moldings, and around doorknobs. Use the roller to cover the flat expanses of wall and ceiling. Though both the brush and the roller require a slight degree of finesse on your part, the brushwork does take a bit more coordination. Decide with your helper who gets to be brushworker and who will be roller operator—or designate and switch!

Just a quick word about the sequence of rolling and brushwork, for both the walls and ceiling. You can do the brushwork first, or the rolling first—or do them both at the same time, if that's how you feel. Which is done first isn't carved in stone, and getting it done is the main thing. I've gotten into the habit of doing it in a certain sequence, however, so I'll describe it in that order, and you can make up your own mind.

STEP 1: *Apply the Primer*

You will decide to either spot-prime or to prime the entire area that will be painted (refer to the section above on primer). You can apply primer with a brush or a roller. If you're covering the entire wall and ceiling area, apply it basically the same way you apply the paint itself (see steps 2 through 4 that follow).

STEP 2: *Do the Ceiling Brushwork*

Generally I start the painting with the ceiling, taking care of the brushwork first. With a 2 ½-inch brush, paint the areas that the roller can't do so well: the inside edge where the ceiling meets the wall, and around any light fixtures. I have done more than one room to the very end before realizing that I forgot to do the brushwork around a ceiling light!

As I mentioned earlier, you should be able to unscrew the cover plate on the ceiling fixture, enabling you to easily paint the ceiling behind it. But if the cover won't come loose, or if loosening it would mean handling a heavy chandelier, you'll find it necessary to do a little careful painting. In this event, take your brush and carefully paint cleanly around the plate. This procedure, in painters' jargon, is called "cutting in." It's quite common in painting

to find a situation in which you have to cut in an edge, carefully painting up to a certain point with your brush without getting paint beyond that line.

If you couldn't get the ceiling light plate to unscrew, then use your brush to cut in the paint around it.

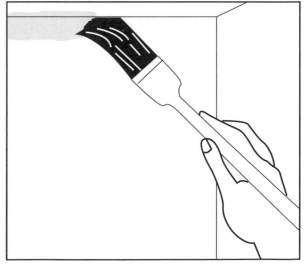

Do the brushwork where the ceiling meets the wall. Going a bit onto the wall is okay.

Don't worry about getting a perfect line where the ceiling and wall meet, because you're going to follow with the wall color anyway. When you do the wall brushwork later, you will try to make a somewhat clean, straight line as you "cut in" the wall paint. (By the way, the reason I start with the ceiling brushwork is because I usually follow right away with the walls, and I want to be sure this part is dry.)

A most important painting tool is a rag. I always check my workmates to be sure they all have a nice absorbent piece of cloth (cotton, as opposed to polyester) hanging from their back pocket. I mean, you can strictly cover and protect your furniture and carpeting and everything else until the room looks like a NASA experiment in germ containment, but the truth is that you still might get a spot of paint on something. But with your rag at the ready, you're prepared to immediately clean it up.

You will probably get your own hang of it as you do the brushwork. But here are a couple of suggestions that might help you out:

- Pour some paint into a cup or large soup can, and work from that. It's easier (and safer) than attempting the daring act of carrying a full can of paint up the ladder with you.

- Each time you dip the brush into the paint, use only the last inch of the bristles to carry that dip of paint. It'll be more manageable, and the paint won't start running up your arm as you reach to get those high spots.

- Wipe the brush off on the inside edge of the can each time before dipping in for a new swipe. This will help keep the bristles straight, unbroken, and clean.

Other than that, just go for it. I've always tried to make sure I get to do the brushwork, because I think it's the most fun.

STEP 3: *Roll the Ceiling and Walls*

Start by rolling the roller handle with the sleeve on it into the paint tray and getting a good amount of paint onto the sleeve—but not so much that it's running all over the place. I usually twirl the roller slowly as I lift it out of the tray over to the area I'm painting. This helps to avoid big drips along the way. You'll soon figure out when you're putting too much paint on the roller, and can scale back if need be.

Concentrate on 4-by-4-foot squares at a time, making a W that size, then filling it in, rolling back and forth. Spread the paint out nice and evenly so there are no thick patches and so that everything within the square is covered. Work your way methodically across the ceiling (left to right, or right to left; from one side to the other). On the walls, you'll find it easy to make top squares and then bottom squares (each 4-by-4) and to work your way along like that.

"Feather" the edges of each square; that is, keep a light touch at the edges, rolling the paint roller lightly to the edges of each square so that there are no thick lines where the squares meet, just solid color.

Now, let me point out that if you are using a flat finish, this is enough to ensure that the final product (your masterpiece) will dry nice and even. If, however, it's an eggshell, satin, or gloss finish (anything with a sheen to it), listen up. There's an added step in the rolling of it that you've got to do, so that when it dries, it dries evenly, not patchy-looking.

After painting the upper and lower squares on the wall, this added step involves re-rolling your finished rectangle (upper and lower square combined). Re-roll each rectangle from bottom to top; there's no need to put new paint on the sleeve. This re-rolling blends everything together and brings the direction of the newly applied paint evenly upward, so that as it dries (and falls with gravity), the resulting sheen will have a uniform look.

Roll the ceiling in squares, feathering the edges as you go along.

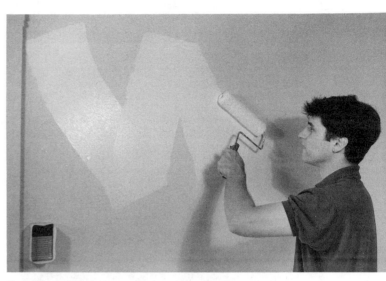

Roll the wall in squares, starting with a W shape.

Roll your W out, filling the square nicely and taking care to spread the paint somewhat evenly.

As you move along the wall, go back to each upper and lower square and lightly roll from top to bottom to ensure that the entire expanse is covered evenly.

Those Popcorn Ceilings

Beware of acoustical ceilings—you know, that popcorn stuff! When the acoustical material was applied, it was sprayed on by a big machine, and sometimes these ceilings are then spray-painted. If your acoustical ceiling was painted, then you may not have a problem trying to repaint it—though chances are that more little particles than you will care to know about will stick to your paint sleeve as you roll the paint on.

But if the ceiling has never been painted or if you live in a damp part of the country, tread carefully! As the pressure of wet paint and roller handle glides across an unpainted acoustical ceiling, you will most likely watch (in horror) as most of the popcorn peels right off, down to the drywall!

Avoid these ceilings if you can. And if they must be painted, do you know a professional who can at least give you advice on your particular ceiling and circumstances?

Now take care of the wall brushwork everywhere you couldn't get at with the roller.

STEP 4: *Do the Wall Brushwork*

Now that you've finished the ceiling brushwork and rolling, and the walls have been rolled, you can do the wall brushwork. You were probably able to roll the wall paint within $1\frac{1}{2}$ inches of all edges (base moldings, window trim, door trim, and the intersection of wall and ceiling). So now with your brush, finish up by carefully cutting in the wall color at the ceiling and next to windows, doors, and molding.

STEP 5: *Apply a Second Coat if Desired*

If the ceiling or the walls need a second coat of paint, just repeat your labors from the first coat. Most of the time, you can apply the second coat right after the first, beginning the second coat back where the first one was started. It isn't really neces-

sary for the first coat to dry totally. Note, though, that coverage of the old paint will be enhanced the longer you wait between coats.

At this point in the project, with all the main wall and ceiling painting done, I take up all the drop cloths and newspapers—anything covering the floor. Some painters leave the drops down until the entire job is finished. By doing an initial sort of straightening up, however, you can check to see if you've gotten paint anywhere and clean it up.

STEP 6: *Paint the Trim*

Now you're ready for the trim, which means base molding, doors and door trim, and window trim and frames. You might even have a crown molding (a strip of decorative wood that runs along the top of

Spot Removal

If you've gotten a bit of oil-based paint on your plush carpet, there are a couple of ways to deal with it. You can let it dry (keeping in mind where it is; be careful not to walk on it), and then cut it out a day later with a sharp razor blade. Or you can try to get it out with one of the "miracle" spot removers that are on the market. These removers generally claim they won't damage or discolor carpeting, and they usually don't. They can work very well—but smell really awful (and I wonder how different they are from nail polish remover, anyway).

If you're unsure of your brushwork capabilities, lay masking tape along the floor at the base of the walls.

the wall at the ceiling). The trim is usually painted in a satin or gloss finish: These finishes are with a sheen, and are especially durable and washable.

While painting the trim, I've always found it easier to protect the floors by simply putting a few new sheets of newspaper under each door, or by carrying a small drop cloth around from one trim area to the next. While you do the trim painting, you can handle on-the-spot cleanup with just a water-moistened rag (for latex paint) or a bit of paint thinner (for oil- and alkyd-based paint).

Base Molding

This part of the job is all done with the brush. As an aid in painting the molding, you can put masking tape on the floor—a trick I've done many times. Most masking tape has to be doubled up to ensure that the paint doesn't bleed through the tape, and even then some of it may, anyway.

If you feel confident about your brushwork, you can skip the masking and just take your time, carefully cutting in the paint at the floor with your brush. On new construction, I usually mask the floor; for the older brownstone buildings, I wing it by cutting in with no masking. If the base molding meets carpeting, however, masking tape is definitely the way to go.

Doors

Before I paint a door, I sometimes remove the doorknobs and strike plate so I don't have to cut in the paint around them. (I put this hardware in a bag, marking it and setting it aside until I'm finished.) It's up to you whether or not you remove the hardware. Unless there's a lot of old paint caked on the rosette of the doorknob, making it tough to remove, it usually turns out to be easier and quicker to take off the hardware before painting.

Protect the floor by putting a few sheets of newspaper under the open door. Wedge the door open by jamming a rolled-up piece of newspaper under it.

You may be able to use the roller, rather than the brush, on the main part of each door. But if the door is composed of different panels, it may be easier to just brush the entire door. Since you're probably using a paint with a sheen (like semi-gloss or gloss),

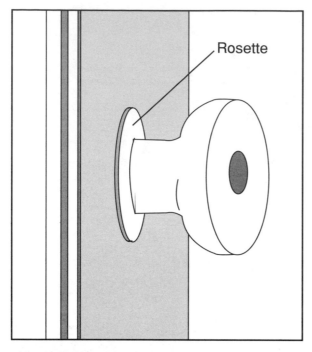

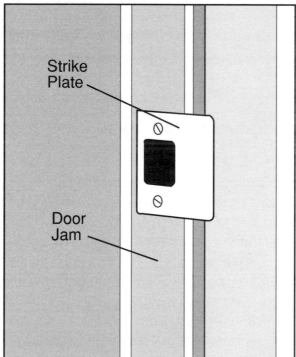

It's usually easier to paint a door if you remove the hardware, like the doorknob (above) and strike plate (below).

complete all the brushing and rolling for each door so that you ensure uniformity in drying. Complete any rolling by doing a clean, continuous bottom-to-top rolling of the surface (remember the wall with the sheen?).

Windows

There are all kinds of windows, and most will require only that you paint the window trim and the window sill. But some windows—especially the old-fashioned double-hung windows—are more complicated. I'll focus here on the double-hung windows, which have both an inside and outside sash (movable window frames).

Begin with the top sash. Pull it down and push the lower sash up, enabling you to paint the bottom part of the top sash. Now push the top sash back up and pull the bottom sash down, so you can paint

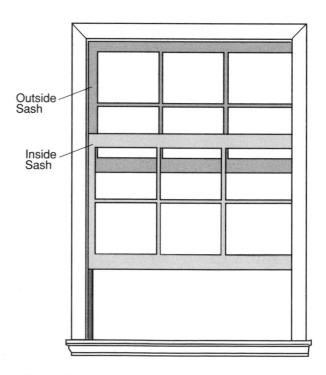

For double-hung windows, paint the outside sash first and then the inside sash, moving them now and then so you avoid painting them shut.

the rest of the top sash. Now you can paint the bottom sash and then the surrounding window jambs and frame.

Some things to keep in mind as you paint these double-hung windows:

- Try not to close the window completely.

- Avoid putting the paint on too thickly.

- Move the sashes up and down occasionally (you don't want to paint the window shut).

- Don't use masking tape on the glass. (It's quicker and easier to just scrape the dried paint off the glass later with a razor blade.)

If you feel that you have a steady hand, cut in the paint where the sash meets the glass. But don't worry if it doesn't come out perfect. It's even OK to paint right onto the glass, maybe half an inch or so as you paint the sashes. This makes it easy to paint the sashes, and ensures that they get painted thoroughly. Then after a day or so (don't wait much longer), use a single-edge razor blade to scrape the glass clean. When you're finished, you'll have very clean lines where wood meets glass.

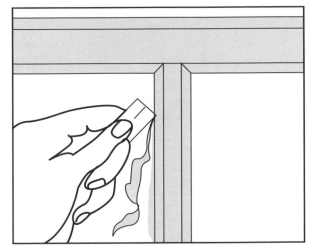

A day or so after painting, the paint can easily be scraped off the glass with a single-edge razor blade.

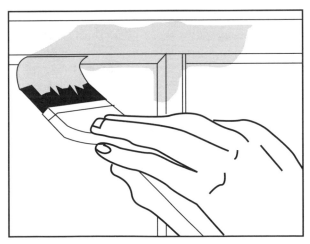

Go ahead and paint right onto the window panes .

THE VOICE OF EXPERIENCE

A Caution About Masking Tape

I always advise against putting masking tape on window glass. Some twenty years back, my dad had just passed away, and my mom was trying to paint the interior of the house. She put masking tape on the window glass to avoid getting paint on it as she painted the sashes. The masking tape got left on for several days before she had time to get back to remove it (she was painting the whole house herself!).

In the meantime, the windows got a good bit of sunlight. The combination of heat and the passage of time created a pretty good bond between the glass and the masking tape. The paper part of the tape would come up, but a stubborn residue of glue stuck to the glass.

I'll never forget how tough it was to clean all those panes of glass! We used mineral spirits to loosen the glue, and then scraped at it with razor blades (lots of them). Ever since then, my advice has been to simply paint the sashes and let the paint slop onto the window glass. After it dries, just go back and scrape the paint off the glass with a razor blade.

STEP 7: *Clean Up*

Cleanup is definitely the best part of the job—the final scraping of paint off the window glass, picking up any newspapers or drop cloths still on the floor, replacing the electrical switch and outlet plates (I hope you took them into the kitchen to clean them, or better yet, bought new ones), and putting the furniture back in place.

Cleanup also means your brushes, your tools, and yourself. If you used oil-based (alkyd-based) paints, the sleeve and the tray liner get tossed. Mineral spirits (or paint thinner, basically the same chemical) will clean your hands and elbows, spots on the floor, and the brush. Dip the brush in a jar of spirits a couple of times, using a putty knife or a small wire brush to scrape off paint that might have caked on the bristles. Then with some clean spirits, rinse it again, wiping it with a clean cloth. You can get the roller handle clean by wiping it with a rag and a little thinner.

If you used a latex (water-based) paint, cleanup is easier because you do the cleaning with water instead of paint thinner. Warm, soapy water works best. To clean the brush, work out most of the paint with your hands as you hold it under running water. Follow up with a putty knife to scrape the outside bristles or any paint that may be a little tough to remove. If the clerk in the hardware store talked you into one of those neat metal combs, run it

through the bristles a few times. These combs, and small wire brushes, work real well in cleaning the bristles. Don't bother trying to clean the roller sleeves; just throw them away. Water and a sponge will clean off spots of paint that may remain elsewhere: on the floor, or in your hair.

Washing Your Sleeves

I don't recommend ever washing a sleeve— also known as a roller or paint applicator— after you've used it. If you try to wash a sleeve, you've got to get the pigment thoroughly out of the nap in order to be able to reuse it. But most sleeves unravel and fall apart before you can get them totally clean. So why bother?

But there is a way to reuse a sleeve, if you are applying latex paint. You can remove the sleeve from the handle, wrap it snugly in a large piece of plastic and make it airtight by sealing with masking tape (or use a Ziploc freezer bag, which works great), and label it. In the airtight plastic, the sleeve and the paint will stay moist, and you can actually reuse the sleeve as much as a year later (with the same color paint, of course). You can also do this with oil paints, though the sleeve is really only reusable for another couple of days.

The Art of Closing a Paint Can

When you put the lid back on a paint can, be kind to yourself or anyone down the line who might have to reopen it. Before you close it, clean any excess paint out of the rim. If you punched nail holes in the rim to allow most of the excess to drip back into the can, then great. But still, be sure the rim is pretty clear of paint before resealing the can. Believe me, it's very difficult to remove a lid from a paint can later on if there is a lot of dried, caked-up paint creating a seal around the rim.

In putting the lid back on, the palm of your hand should be enough pressure around the top of the lid to press it firmly in place. If you want to pound it on with a hammer, be sure to cover the top with a rag; paint will splatter far!

INTERIOR PAINTING AT A GLANCE

PREPARING TO PAINT

MATERIALS CHECKLIST

☐ Putty knife (3-inch-wide blade)

☐ Putty knife (6-inch to 10-inch blade)

☐ Plaster (drywall compound; joint compound; Spackle)

☐ Drywall tape (joint tape)

☐ Drywall (small pieces)

☐ Tube of caulk

☐ Caulking gun

☐ Paint remover (optional)

☐ Wallpaper remover (optional)

☐ Electric wallpaper steamer (optional)

☐ Canvas drop cloths

☐ Plastic drop cloths

☐ Newspaper

☐ Rags

☐ Large sponge

☐ Trisodium phosphate (TSP cleaning solution)

☐ Sandpaper

☐ Single-edge razor blades

☐ Rubber gloves

☐ Screwdrivers

☐ Wire brush

☐ Keyhole saw (or steak knife)

☐ Bucket

☐ Stepladder

THE BASIC STEPS

1. Clear the area by moving furniture out of the way and putting down drop cloths.

2. Remove old wallpaper.

3. Remove paint buildup and loose paint.

4. Repair cracks, holes, and uneven surfaces with plaster, drywall tape, and caulk.

5. Repair the larger holes with plaster and pieces of drywall.

6. Start out clean for painting by dusting walls and cleaning kitchen and bathroom surfaces.

PAINTING

MATERIALS CHECKLIST

☐ Primer

☐ Paint

☐ Pure-bristle paintbrush (for oil- and alkyd-based paint)

☐ Synthetic-bristle paintbrush (tynex or polyester; for latex paints)

☐ Paint tray

☐ Paint tray liners

☐ Roller handle

☐ Sleeves (rollers)

☐ Drop cloths (canvas and/or plastic

☐ Newspaper

☐ Rags

☐ Stepladder

☐ Masking tape

☐ Single-edge razor blades

☐ Screwdriver (regular)

☐ Mineral spirits (paint thinner)

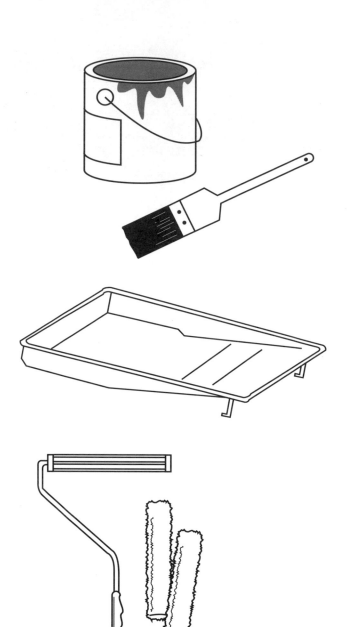

THE BASIC STEPS

1. Apply a primer coat, or spot-prime.

2. Do the ceiling brushwork.

3. Paint the ceiling and walls using the roller.

4. Do the wall brushwork.

5. Follow with a second coat of paint if desired.

6. Paint the trim (such as base molding, doors and door trim, window trim and frames).

7. Clean up.

WALLPAPERING

O f all the things I do now in my home improvement business, I'd have to say hanging wallpaper gives me the most pleasure and satisfaction. The transformation of a room can be spectacular. There are so many wonderful patterns out there—American heritage designs, French provincial, Polo, English garden, country kitchen, and many more. A well-stocked wallpaper store has hundreds of books, each containing hundreds of patterns.

Like paint, a dark wallpaper—or a bold or large pattern—can make a room seem smaller, but it can also give it a cozy feeling. A soft pattern can comfort and soothe. A strong pattern can define a room. A vertical stripe will make walls look taller, and can add a touch of class.

If the room is a kitchen or bathroom, it will be a bit more difficult to hang than, say, a den or living room. But don't let that deter you, please. Bathrooms, especially, have a lot more corners and wall edges than other rooms. This, I think, really just calls for more patience, and you'll be fine. The principles (that is, gluing and putting each piece in place) are basically the same; smaller rooms just call for more cuts with the razor blade. The colors of bathroom tile can be brought out beautifully with a well-chosen paper.

A CLOSE LOOK AT WALLPAPER

Wallpaper not only comes in a lot of patterns, but also in a lot of sizes. A single roll of wallpaper today measures about 36 square feet: typically between 13 and 15 feet long and roughly 27 inches wide (depending on the length of the roll). If you're papering an 8-foot-high wall with a roll that is 13 feet long, you're going to end up with 5 feet of waste. (It's waste, because most patterns require a solid, uninterrupted piece per length of wall.)

So, as a way to offer consumers more continuous footage, without a break, wallpaper is now available in double rolls (also called bolts) and triple rolls. There's just one occasional hitch: Watch out for triple rolls that have two or more strips of wallpaper inside rather than the single unbroken strip that you're looking for.

Wallpaper costs more than paint, unless you find an incredible close-out bargain. Even though a paper may be packaged in double or triple rolls, the price is usually listed per roll, typically $10 to $30 a roll. (So a double roll selling for $20 a roll would cost $40.) A hand-painted designer paper can go for a

THE VOICE OF EXPERIENCE

A Good Deal

At a tag sale in San Francisco, I found three double rolls of a cream-colored wallpaper with ducks printed on it. They were asking a dollar each. I offered $2.50 for the lot. Although I couldn't quite figure where I would hang this stuff, I felt compelled to buy it (I mean, such a deal!). Then I found out that the proceeds from the sale were going to a nearby AIDS shelter. (I felt guilty and gave them $5.00 instead.)

couple hundred dollars a roll (and it's generally sold by the square foot).

A WALLPAPER VOCABULARY

First off, there are a few wallpaper vocabulary words and phrases that you might want to know.

A **REPEAT** is a portion of the pattern that does just that: repeats itself on the paper periodically, from top to bottom. A 9-inch repeat is common, although

double that (18-inch repeats) happens too. I've hung papers with 27-inch repeats, though that is the least common.

One way to categorize wallpapers is by the way their patterns match up as you hang adjoining strips.

A repeat

A **STRAIGHT MATCH** (or set match) has a pattern that repeats at the same level across the face of the paper. This makes it easy to line each successive strip on the wall with the preceding one.

A straight match

A **DROP PATTERN** has a repeat that—in order to line up one piece of paper on the wall with the one next to it—requires you to drop the piece a bit. In other words, the repeat on the left side of one piece of paper will line up with the repeat on the right side of the adjoining piece only if you drop each successive piece the proper distance. If your repeat is every 9 inches on a drop pattern, then usually the required drop distance is $4\frac{1}{2}$ inches, or half the repeat. With this kind of pattern, you need to figure in a bigger waste factor when making your purchase (roughly 10 to 15 percent more than a generous estimate for a straight-match pattern).

A drop pattern

A **RANDOM PATTERN,** which has no repeat at all, is the easiest to hang. Vertical stripes fall into this category. And because no part of one piece needs to be matched to the next, there is very little waste. (Sample next page)

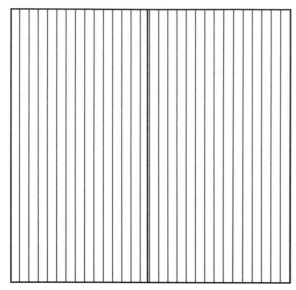

A random pattern

TYPES OF WALLPAPER

There are all kinds of coverings you can put on your walls (and ceilings). I may refer to them all as wallpaper (out of habit), but bear in mind that only some of them are actually made of paper.

Standard Wallpapers

Standard papers are composed of a paper front and paper backing. They can require some patience to work with, especially for the first-time paperhanger, because they are sensitive and tend to tear easily when wet, making them somewhat difficult to hang. (Think about it: You're applying several pounds of wet glue to a long piece of paper, and then holding it up by the corners.)

The coating on the pattern may or may not be waterproof, but in either case it will scratch quite easily after it is in place on a wall. (Some of these papers have a light vinyl coating, making them a bit more durable.)

The nice thing about working with standard papers is that they stick to themselves just fine. If you intentionally overlap seams, or just can't learn to get the seams to lie perfectly and one edge sits over the other a little, it's OK; it'll stick. This is a definite advantage in corners, where you want to overlap somewhat to ensure that the piece coming out of the corner onto the adjoining wall continues to be level.

Standard papers also have a bit of "give" and can be stretched slightly if necessary as you try to butt the seams during hanging.

Because standard papers damage easily, they are best used for ceilings, for walls in relatively formal rooms such as the living room or dining room, or maybe the walls in an adult's bedroom.

Vinyls

The most common wall coverings are the vinyls. They are the easiest to hang, are durable, and don't scratch easily. They don't crease and crumple as readily as the standard papers while you are hanging them. They can have a paper backing, vinyl backing, or, as with some industrial papers, be held together with cloth mesh.

Because they're made of rubber-like fibers, the vinyls hold up well to water. This is a real plus, especially if you're using the prepasted variety, which has to survive being submerged in a bucket of water and later wiped down with wet sponges.

There are a couple of drawbacks to vinyls in comparison with the standard papers. Vinyls cannot be stretched. And the edges must be butted against each other with no overlapping seams. You see, vinyl does not stick to vinyl and so must lie on the wall surface for proper adhesion. If a seam overlaps even slightly, the outer edge will stick out, away from the wall.

At corners (or if a separate border is to be hung over the vinyl), a special border/seam adhesive is needed. And even if you use the adhesive to hold down an overlapped seam, the lap will probably be more apparent than with standard papers because vinyls are usually thicker.

Because vinyl wall coverings are highly durable and washable, they're great for bathrooms, kitchens, kids' rooms, or any high-traffic area.

Grasscloth

Grasscloths are generally pretty easy to hang. They're a thick woven paper with a paper backing. They don't have a pattern to them, and they were a big hit in the seventies.

Flocks

Flocks (also called embossed papers) are papers with a raised pattern, usually in velveteen. They were very common in the Victorian era. Modern versions are backed with paper, vinyl, or cloth. In San Francisco today, it's common to see a raised pattern installed between the base molding and the chair rail (a horizontal wall molding about 32 inches from the floor). This raised-pattern, uncolored paper is called anaglypta. Once in place, it's painted (usually in a glossy finish) to create a wainscoting (the term used to describe the entire section: base, painted anaglypta, and chair rail).

Embossed papers are often hung between a chair rail and base moldings to create a wainscoting.

PREPASTED WALLPAPER VS. REGULAR WALLPAPER

Among the various kinds of wall coverings, there is a choice between prepasted or regular papers (on which you brush the glue). Prepasted coverings have the adhesive already on the back of the paper, in dry form. When you're ready to hang the paper, you dip each strip into water to activate the glue.

The prepasted experience is an all-around easier method for the beginner, basically because it eliminates the glue-application step. Prepasted papers are the most common ones you'll find at the wallpaper store, although many papers (especially the more expensive coverings) still come glueless.

The glueless wallpapers have at least one advantage over the prepasted versions. Once you've wet the back of the prepasted paper, you've got to move right along with the hanging, or else the activated glue will dry out. On the other hand, applying the glue with a brush is more forgiving, and allows you more time for hanging. Professional paperhangers usually prefer applying their own glue because it gives them more control over the work.

I find that brushing on the glue and putting up the paper as in the old days can be pretty enjoyable. It takes me a little longer to hang a room with regular paper, but I have to say that I get more satisfaction out of the experience.

Later in this chapter, I'll go through, step-by-step, both procedures: hanging a prepasted wallpaper and hanging a regular wallpaper.

WALLPAPER GLUE

For wallpapers that are not prepasted, there are a couple of different kinds of glues. In the old days, they were all made from components of wheat germ. Eventually synthetic materials (like cellulose) were developed.

Labeling on the box or can of adhesives is pretty straightforward: "lightweight," "medium to heavyweight," or "heavyweight." Common sense will tell you that the lightweight glues would be best for very light papers. Medium weight translates to most vinyls, although heavyweight glues are also used for many vinyls that are vinyl-backed. "Mildew resistant for vinyls" will be clearly noted on the fronts of labels.

You can buy wallpaper glue either premixed or in powder form that you mix yourself. The premixed is a bit more expensive. How much will you need? Get the adhesive in the same place as the paper, and the salesperson should be able to tell you how much is needed. For hanging eight rolls of wallpaper, for instance, you might need about a pound of dry adhesive or two gallons of premixed.

CHOOSING A PATTERN

As I mentioned earlier, wall-covering in a room can transform it into a wonderful place. A flower pattern adds a soft appearance. Vertical stripes make the walls "taller." Papering the ceiling makes the room cozier.

Choosing a pattern is all a matter of personal taste. Unless you can afford a designer (and are willing to let someone else choose for you!), just head to the wallpaper store. Look through the sample books and at the stock on the walls, and something is bound to hit you—or at least get you interested.

As your taste begins to give you indications of what you'd like to see up on your own walls, set aside those patterns that you feel interested in. Almost always, the clerk will cut you a small swatch from the corner of each page that you like, to take home. This will give you a chance to think about it, to compare it to your furniture, curtains, and other fabrics and colors in the room, and to show your friends or family.

HOW MUCH PAPER WILL I NEED?

To find the square footage of the surfaces to be papered, you will need a tape measure and a pencil (you don't really need paper; just write on the wall). Start with one wall, and work your way clockwise around the room (or counterclockwise, if you feel more comfortable). Multiply the height times the width, treating the wall like a solid surface, even if there is a door or window (that is, don't make allowances for them).

And overestimate. For instance, if the height of a wall is 5 feet, 4 inches, then call it an even 6 feet. Or if the height is 7 feet, 9 inches, call it 8 feet. The point is, you want to end up with more paper, to cover your waste factor. Once you've decided upon the paper, bought it, and brought it home, you don't want to run out midway through the job (believe me). You'll have glue sitting out, and on your shirt, and the store may have sold out of your pattern. Or worse, it may have originally have had to be ordered, and that may have taken two or three weeks (and you'll want to put the furniture back). So include all the wall (or ceiling) surfaces that you plan to cover. Add your figures up, and, voila!, you now have your square footage.

Buying the Paper

As I mentioned earlier, wall coverings may come in double rolls or triple rolls, or may even be sold by the yard from a huge stock roll (maybe, if you've chosen an extremely expensive wall covering). On top of that, an "English roll" contains almost half the square footage of an American roll. Or the pattern you like may come in a 36-inch width and be packaged for commercial use (further confusing you and me).

So bring that number, your square footage needed, to the wallpaper store. First thing is to find a pattern that you like. On the back of the chosen swatch will be the information on how that particular pattern is packaged; for example, "double rolls, 57.5

square feet." In this case, if your square footage was 205, you'd need four of those double rolls (four would give you 230 square feet, while three would cover only 172 square feet). Or ask the salesperson to tally how much you need.

PREPARATIONS FOR WALLPAPERING

The prep work includes getting any painting out of the way and then repairing and maybe "sizing" (I'll explain this below) the surfaces to be wallpapered.

TOOLS AND MATERIALS

For preparing and "sizing" the walls, here is what you will need.

- Putty knife (6-inch blade or wider)
- Wallpaper size
- Paint tray
- Paint roller handle and sleeve
- Paintbrush
- Mixing bucket
- Drop cloths
- Sandpaper
- Stepladder
- Plaster (drywall compound; joint compound; Spackle)
- Primer

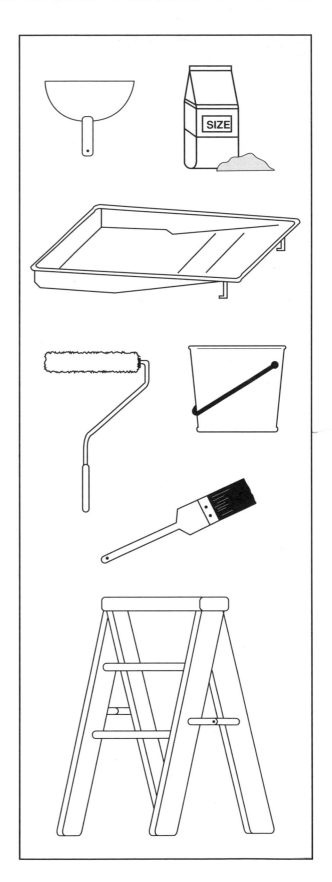

Find a Helper

Hanging wallpaper is so much more enjoyable (and a heck of a lot easier) when done with a helper. Do you have a friend or relative (mother, son, wife, husband) to help with the work? The process of wallpapering calls for a lot of different steps, as you'll see, all to be executed while the glue is wet on the back of a strip of wallpaper. Whenever I have a helper, it really does go a lot smoother than if I were working by myself. If you both can familiarize yourselves with what's got to be done, you can designate tasks to each other.

PREPARATIONS, STEP BY STEP

STEP 1: *Clear the Area*

Clear the room of as much stuff as you can. Move furniture away from the walls and use drop cloths to protect the furniture and floor. (Take a look at the section called "Preparations for Painting" in Chapter 1, the chapter on painting, for details on clearing the area.)

STEP 2: *Paint First*

OK, you've decided which room needs wallpaper. If the trim or ceiling needs to be painted, now would be a good time, before the wall covering is hung. The nice thing is that you don't have to be careful with the paint at places where these newly painted surfaces come in contact with the walls to be papered. You won't have to carefully cut in at the place, say, where the base molding meets up with the wall, saving you some labor time.

Actually, if you are painting the base, it's more helpful to paint up on the wall a little less than an inch. This will ensure that, even if your trimming of

the wallpaper in that spot isn't perfect, no old wall color will show after the room has been painted and papered.

If you do have to get any painting done, and you're going with a latex (water-based) product, you ought to figure on giving the area a good week between painting and the time you commence hanging. There's going to be a lot of wetness going on—water-based glue; wet, sopping sponges—that could loosen a latex paint if it came in contact with the papering too soon. If you use an alkyd-based paint, a wait of two or three days should be enough.

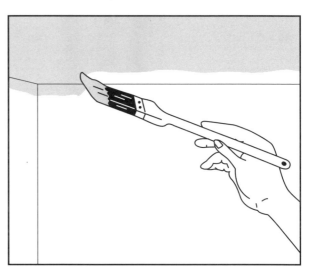

If you're painting the ceiling or trim before hanging your paper, let the paint run onto the surface that the wallpaper will cover.

STEP 3: *Repair and Smooth the Walls*

Though wallpaper is touted as being able to cover a multitude of sins, it still needs a clean, smooth surface as a base if it is to look its best. Wallpaper with a lot of pattern tends to camouflage an irregular wall surface, while dark and light solids tend to highlight bad walls.

In any case, the surfaces should be ready to hold the paper. All this work you're going to, you want the paper to stick on the wall, right? Fill cracks, crevices, and areas where paint has peeled with some sort of plaster (joint compound, drywall compound, Spackle). Patch any large cracks or holes (see the section on wall repair in Chapter 1, the chapter on painting). Paint over the repaired areas with primer.

If the old paint on the walls is glossy or semi-glossy, run some sandpaper over it. No need to use a lot of elbow grease. You're just trying to dull the surface a bit to help the glue adhere better. If there are bumps, sand them down too.

Be sure there are no little "nibs" on the walls anywhere (you know, those tiny pieces of debris that might have been rolled on with the paint). Though relatively unseen on painted surfaces, they will show once wallpaper is glued over them, creating a distressing little raised point.

To be sure I haven't missed any spots while sanding, I'll take a scraper with a blade at least 6 inches wide and run it across the surfaces to knock off any unseen nibs. While doing this, I run my other hand over the wall, feeling for more nibs, which are sometimes easier to feel than to see.

STEP 4: *Consider "Sizing" the Walls*

At this point, the surfaces have been repaired (if necessary) and spot-primed, any glossy paint has been dulled, and the nibs have been scraped off. It's possible that the surfaces are now ready for the wallpaper. First, though, consider whether you should put a coat of "sizing" on the wall to give a better base for the paper.

If the walls you will be papering have a flat-finish paint on them, your hanging will go more smoothly if you apply sizing to the wall. Size is a clear, water-based coating that's painted on to give the wall surfaces uniformity and a slight sheen. It enables you to slide glued pieces of paper into place more easily than over the flat paint itself. Sizing is inexpensive and is generally sold in powder form. Mix it up and apply it to the walls just like paint, using a paint roller.

In general, it is simply a good idea to size the walls. But I admit that I have skipped this step at times. If, for instance, the walls had just been primed (most primers have a slight sheen to them), I'd move right on to the paperhanging.

If you're a little "iffy" about whether to size the walls, you might as well do it. It requires little time, and it will help you later as you try to adjust a strip of paper on the wall. The sizing dries quickly; the paperhanging can commence just a few hours after sizing, if you'd like.

HANGING PREPASTED WALLPAPER

Prepasted wall coverings tend to be the most popular for do-it-yourselfers, and certainly for first-timers. Whether you use a prepasted paper or the type that requires you to apply the glue, the steps for hanging are basically the same. The only difference between the two is how you deal with the adhesive in each case—and I'll explain that thoroughly in this chapter.

TOOLS AND MATERIALS

Following are the tools and materials needed for hanging prepasted wallpaper.

- Wallpaper
- Putty knife (minimum 6-inch-wide blade)
- Smoothing brush (or smoothing knife)
- Two large sponges
- Seam roller (seamer)
- Border/seam adhesive (for vinyl paper)
- Level
- Tape measure
- Pencil

- Single-edge razor blades
- Drop cloths
- Stepladder
- Water tray
- Trash bag

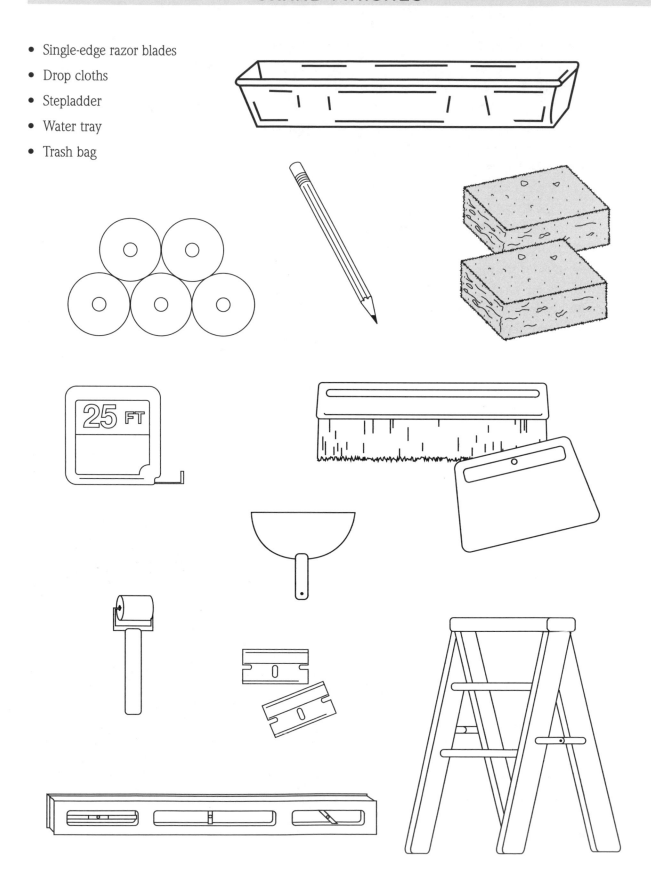

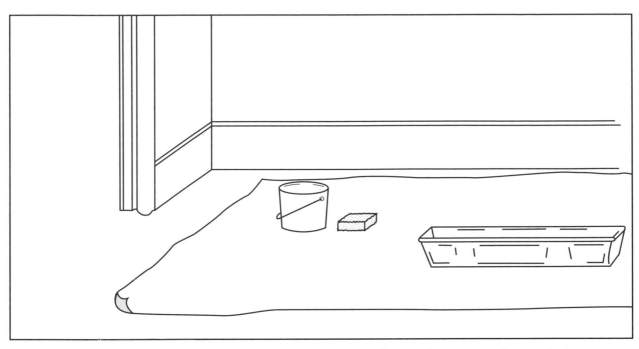

Set up your workstation on a canvas dropcloth or old sheet, giving yourself plenty of room to wet the strips in the water tray.

CUT SOME PIECES IN ADVANCE

I usually cut at least 70 percent of my pieces ahead of time, for two reasons. One, I like to be prepared. And two, it's easier to not have to do a lot of cutting once the actual paperhanging has begun and there's glue and water everywhere.

Precutting is not essential. If you're a bit insecure about this step, then by all means wait and cut each piece as you need it. You can take many breaks during paperhanging, even in the middle of a wall. Unlike painting, you don't have to finish one whole wall without stopping.

Make a Mark

Decide which way is up, for your pattern. Whether you decide to cut several pieces in advance or one piece at a time, make a pencil mark at the top of each piece, on the back side. Use pencil, mind you: the ink from a pen will bleed through wet paper. Once you're up on the ladder with a gluey piece of

Cut your strips of wallpaper ahead of time, or at least in a dry area as you go along.

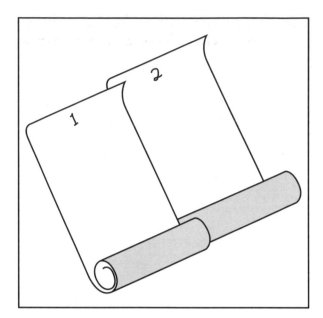

Make it easy on yourself—identify each strip with a pencil mark on the top of the nonpatterned side.

patterned paper, it's not always obvious which end should go up. I find it helps to mark either the length of that particular piece (say 8'6") or the order in which you plan to hang the pieces (1, 2, 3). Or maybe they'll all end up being the same length, in which case any old mark will do.

Pay Attention to the Pattern

It's important that you notice what kind of pattern you have as you cut each piece to length. The way the pattern on a piece will line up to the next piece on the wall should be taken into account now. Let me explain.

RANDOM PATTERN

This pattern doesn't repeat. Hooray! You won't have to worry about matching the pattern as you hang piece after piece on the wall.

So your precut strips of a random pattern really only need an extra few inches at top and at the bottom. For example, if the distance between the base and the ceiling is 8 feet, 3 inches, cut your strips to just under 9 feet. This will give you a 3- or 4-inch

excess at the top and the bottom. This extra will get cut off once a piece is hung, but it's good to have, just in case of error (such as your cut not being completely straight).

STRAIGHT-MATCH PATTERN (SET MATCH)

The straight-match does have a repeat in the pattern. Remember, this is the most common one: each repeat lines up from one side of the paper to the other.

Find how often the pattern repeats by looking for an identifiable image at the edge of the paper. Look farther down the edge to find where you see it again. Could be every 9 inches (very common), every 4 1/2 inches, or even every inch.

Being that I talk to myself, I give that identifiable image a name for the really abstract patterns. Whatever it looks like at first glance, like "birdie lying sideways" or "birdie with a big head." This way I can spot each repeating "picture" easily (and say it aloud to keep myself company).

If the distance between repeats is 9 inches or more, figure on giving yourself at least a foot of "safety" per strip when you do your cutting. In other words, allow an extra 6 inches at the top and the bottom. And also be sure that the repeat starts at about the same place, at the top of each new piece, as you cut from the roll.

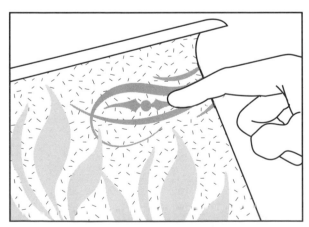

For abstract patterns, find an obvious identifiable portion of the pattern that you can find easily; this will help you match the pattern.

DROP PATTERN

The one to pay attention to the most is the drop pattern. Again, pick out an identifiable part of the pattern to use as your reference point. When the strips of wallpaper are lined up and hung on the wall, this identifiable part will seem to drop from one strip to the next (usually half the distance of the repeat). In other words, the repeat on the left side of the strip won't match up directly across on the right side, as it does in the straight-match pattern.

Looking at the wall, cut your strips so that each succeeding piece that will be hung starts at a point that will match up the repeat of the previous piece. Again, give an extra 6 inches or so at the top and the bottom of each piece.

If I've got to cut, say, ten pieces all the same length to go across a wall, I'll label the first one "A" (in pencil, on the back at the top), the second one "B," the third one "A," and so on. The reason is that with a drop pattern, the first piece is almost always like the third, and the second like the fourth, as far as where the repeat appears at the top of the piece so that everything lines up.

PAPERHANGING, STEP BY STEP

STEP 1: *Draw a Plumb Line on the Wall*

The first thing to do would probably be to figure out where you'd like to begin. An inconspicuous corner is always good. Let's say, then, that your wall covering is 20½ inches wide. Measure out a bit more than that (say 21 inches) from the corner, and draw a vertical line at that point with your level. This line will be your guide, to help ensure that the first piece you hang is straight as you put it up on the wall.

No house is perfectly plumb, with all corners being exactly 90 degrees and all floors and ceilings perfectly level. So if you repeat the procedure of drawing a plumb line on the wall each time you turn a corner, you'll end up with a straight job.

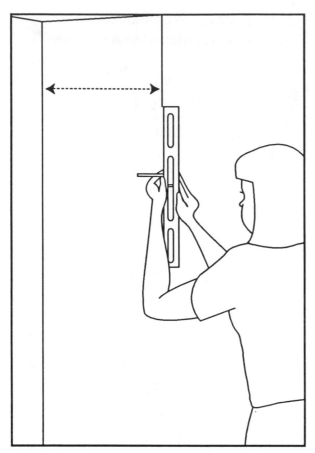

Measure out from your starting point about a half inch more than the width of your paper and draw a plumb line in pencil to use as a guide.

Pull the wet piece out of the water tray, being careful not to tear the edges, and fold it over onto itself, glue facing glue.

STEP 2: *Activate the Glue*

As you know, the only real difference between prepasted papers and regular (glue-application) papers is what you have to go through to get the adhesive ready and wet. With prepasted papers, the adhesive is already on the back, in dry form. It just needs to be activated.

To activate, place the first dry strip of paper on the floor between you and the water tray. Begin to unroll it by taking an end of the strip and submerging it in the water. Slowly feed the entire strip into the water and basically reroll it into the water tray. Use your fingers to ease the strip into the water, with your thumbs acting on either side of the piece as guide.

Be sure the entire back side of the strip gets wet as you feed it into the water. If there are any air pockets, obviously the glue won't be activated there, and that part won't stick to the wall.

The piece is totally submerged. So now, by holding the piece at the very ends of the corners, pull it up out of the water. Give it a second or two to let the excess water drip down. To avoid getting gluey water everywhere, stand pretty much over the tray.

Unless you're eight feet tall, you'll only be able to pull a little more than half of the piece out of the water. Carefully (this may take a bit of practice) let the first part of the paper fall over the back side evenly, so that the glue side is back-to-back with itself. Then reach down, lightly grasp the piece evenly by the sides, and pull the remainder of the strip out of the water.

Now carefully lay the half-folded, half-open piece

on the drop-clothed area or on a table. Fold the open half of the strip over on itself, glue-to-glue, just like the first half you pulled out. This is called booking the piece. What you're doing is basically putting the piece into a more manageable package, as well as giving the activated glue a chance to, well, become activated. Hopefully the booked piece has no glued back side showing; it should all be folded onto itself. (For more on booking a piece of glued wallpaper, see pages 57–59.)

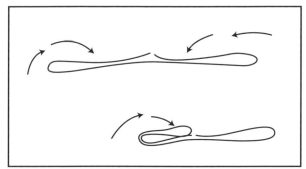

Booking the piece: After you pull the wet strip up out of the water tray, fold each end into the center, glue side to glue side, lining up the edges; then fold the new ends into the center again.

STEP 3: *Hang the First Piece*

Place the stepladder in front of the wall space where the first piece is to go. Gingerly carry the wet, sopping, glue-activated booked piece over to the wall. Peel open the top part (you put a pencil mark on the top back side of the piece, right?). Standing on the ladder and holding the piece by the upper corners, hold it up at the wall. OK, if this is the right spot and your plumb line shows that the piece is straight, place it up on the wall.

Allow at least three extra inches of paper on the top, past the ceiling, and maybe half an inch or an inch on the side into and past the corner. You'll find that the piece will slide a bit if you have to adjust it. (Or if you have to pull the piece up off the wall and lay it down again, you can do that.) With the top part

of the paper pushed against the wall, let the booked bottom half unfold and hang down. Gently smooth that piece onto the wall, down to the base molding.

Carry the first strip over to the wall and line it up with your plumb line.

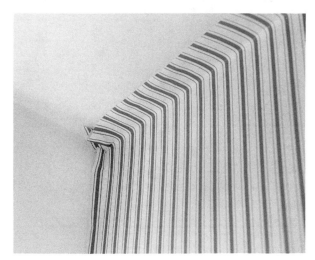

Crease the piece into the corner at the wall and ceiling.

STEP 4: *Smooth and Sponge*

Now, in a cross pattern, moving outward from the center, smooth the piece in place, flat onto the wall. Use either your smoothing brush or smoothing knife. Don't be too aggressive or forceful with the covering. Your aim is to push all the bubbles out from beneath the paper—but you don't want to wrinkle, stretch, or crease it.

As soon as you've got it smoothed in place, take a clean, wet sponge and wipe the front of the paper. This serves two purposes. It cleans any glue residue that may have found its way onto the front, either when the sheet was rolled in the water tray or when glue was pushed out the sides from the back during smoothing. And it continues to smooth out any bubbles you may have missed the first time around.

Rinse out the sponge frequently during the cleaning of each piece (maybe two or three times). If the glue isn't cleaned out of the sponge often, you're really just spreading thinned-out glue onto the front of the paper. This is important: even the slightest amount left on the paper will show up when dry. And then it's not as easy to clean off.

STEP 5: *Trim Off the Excess Paper*

Now grab the wide putty knife. Hold it up at the ceiling with the blade sitting in the corner where wall and ceiling meet. With a single-edge razor blade, cut the excess off the top of the piece, using the putty-knife blade as a guide. As you cut, carefully slide the blade (still in the corner) along the piece. Do the same at the bottom, this time placing the putty knife blade at the junction where the wall meets the base molding.

This isn't a bad time to clean off any glue that got on the ceiling or base molding.

Smooth the piece into place, forcing out any bubbles and being careful not to crease or wrinkle the face of the sheet.

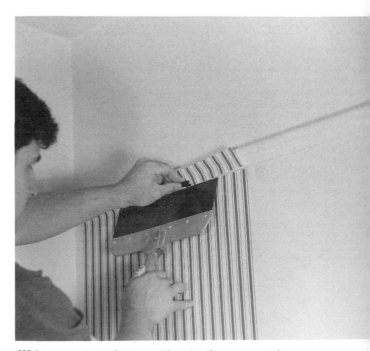

With your putty knife as a guide, trim the excess at the top and bottom of each strip.

Keeping It Neat

Keep your trash bag close by as you cut the excess off the strips of wallpaper you've just hung. I've been called neat, even "anal," by my clients, but each piece of excess wet wallpaper immediately gets folded up and thrown into the trash bag. Otherwise I'd have pieces everywhere and glue drying in places I don't need it to dry. Worse, I could end up stepping on the gluey pieces. (I hate walking around with something stuck to the bottom of my shoe!)

STEP 6: *Smooth the Edges Down*

Take the seam roller and run it up and down the edge of the paper. This will give you further assurance that the piece will stick to the wall.

Wipe the front of the paper with a freshly rinsed sponge. I always feel you can't clean the front of the wall covering enough. Most glues are clear, and when they and the paper you're working on are

wet, it's almost impossible to tell if there is any residue on the paper. Frequent wipings will give you a good chance of getting rid of this glue. As I've mentioned, it's not easy to remove residue after the paper dries. You can buy a dried-glue remover—but it's always nicer to have the job really done when it's done, know what I mean?

STEP 7: *Hang the Next Strip (and the Next)*

Now roll your second strip into the water tray, activating the glue. Pull it out and book it. If you want to take it one piece at a time, then by all means, do. Once you get comfortable with your new skill, however, it won't hurt to have two or even three pieces wet and booked at a time. Actual papers, versus vinyls, tend to require a little more glue-activation time (sitting in booked position), so it may even be advisable to have at least one booked piece ready and waiting as you work on hanging another.

Judge your own rhythm, though. Once a prepasted strip is activated, it will begin to dry out slowly. No matter how agile you may become, having more than three pieces activated at a time is probably pushing it.

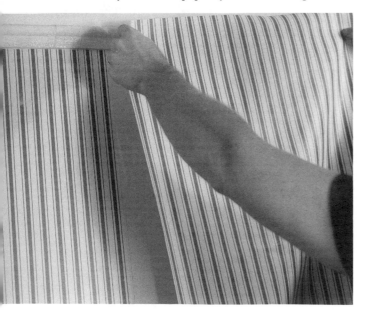

Hang your second strip the same way as the first, this time lining up the edges.

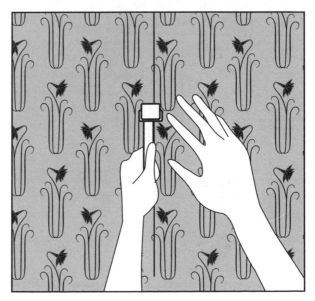

Where the two edges meet, roll the seam with your seam roller.

Anyway, move your ladder over to where the new piece is going to go, next to the piece you hung earlier. Open the top end of the second strip so you can hold it by the top corners. Bring it over to the wall, and let it fall open. Line up the pattern at the edges of the two pieces to create a seam as close together as possible without overlapping.

Smooth this new strip out, as you did the first piece, this time first paying special attention to how the edges meet to form a seam and then completely smoothing the piece in place. I use the smoothing brush for really sensitive papers or foils, but for most other coverings—especially vinyls—I've become a convert to the plastic smoothing knife. Carefully used, it enables you to push the very edge of the paper to the left or the right to get a perfectly matched and butted seam. I feel it gives you much more control than the traditional smoothing brush. (Of course, with control comes power—and it's much easier to cause a wrinkle or crease with the plastic smoothing knife if you get a bit careless.)

Be sure the edges sit nicely before trimming the excess off the second piece. If necessary, lift or slide the strip to where you want it.

THE VOICE OF EXPERIENCE

A Question of Overlap

Some instruction manuals suggest that you slightly overlap wallpapers, or that you bring the edges of vinyls together so that the seams are raised slightly. The reasoning in both cases is that as the wallpapers dry, they will pull back just a bit and leave a fine seam.

I have to say that I've had the best luck by just trying to line up my seams as best as I can: not overlapping, but just butting the edges to each other. Wallpapers do tend to shrink a bit, but really not so much as to merit overlapping at the seams.

Now follow the same steps with this piece as you did with the first one. Smooth out bubbles; clean, clean, clean the front of the piece; trim the extra stuff off the top and bottom; run the seam roller along the edges.

One thing that I've noticed when hanging a wallpaper that has paper backing. Sometimes these papers will show a lot of small bubbles when they're first put on the wall. You can smooth and smooth, yet there they still are. Don't worry: chances are that most of them will flatten out and disappear once the paper and glue begin to dry. (Take another look back at the first piece after you've hung four or five strips, and resmooth with the sponge then.)

At this point, two pieces are up. You can now proceed to cover the rest of the wall. Hang piece after piece, and follow the same procedures.

STEP 8: *Cut Around Windows and Doors*

As you go along, hanging each new piece pretty much the same as the last, you will eventually come to a window or door. Even cutting around these openings, the paperhanging techniques are basically the same.

As you approach a window, continue to line the edge of the newest piece up to the edge of the strip that preceded it, and begin the smoothing process. At the window, smooth the side of the piece right up to the closest edge of the window casing, or trim.

At the very top corner of the trim—which you should be able to feel through the paper with your finger—stick a sharp razor blade in, and pull it diagonally down into the space of the window. Make that cut all the way to the other side of the paper. This will allow the paper to now hug the top and side of the window trim and be smoothed snugly to the wall.

Now do the same at the bottom corner of the window trim. Feel through the paper with your finger to find the exact corner. Again, stick in a sharp razor blade, and pull it diagonally up into the window space, again cutting all the way to the other side of the paper.

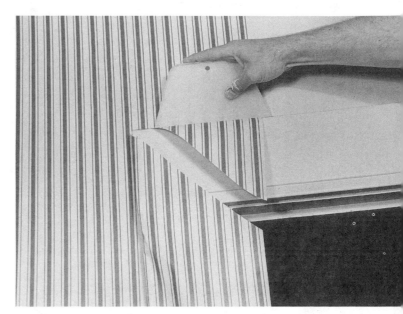

Make a diagonal cut in the direction of the door frame so you can smooth the piece all the way to the door casing on the sides as well as the top.

When you come to a door frame, smooth the piece down along the side edge of the door casing.

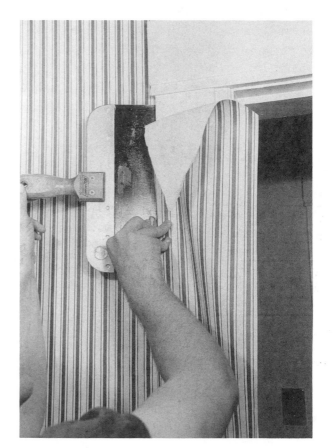

With your putty knife and razor blade, cut away the excess paper along the door casing.

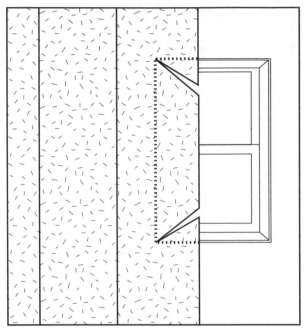

Using your putty knife as a guide, trim the excess around the door casing.

A SPECIAL NOTE: If the molding under your window sill is not just a simple corner but is multi-tiered, be careful to not cut off too much paper. Instead of only one cut, you'll want to make several cuts, close to one another—all the while feeling the

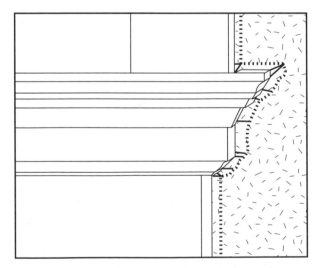

Carefully make cuts (like the simple single diagonal cut toward the door frame) at each edge of sill casing to free the piece along the molding edge and give you enough guide to trim the piece.

paper pressed up to the side of the molding, and allowing it to guide your cutting.

Now that the paper is smoothed on the wall to the perimeter of the window molding, you can cut off the excess with your razor blade and putty knife, just as you would at the base molding and the ceiling. Give the window trim a good wiping with a clean, wet sponge, as you've been doing with the fronts of each piece of paper, the ceiling, and the base molding.

Chances are that this first window piece, once hung, won't "pass" the window (that is, it won't reach to the open wall surface on the other side). The next piece, which will probably "cover" the window completely, may be a bit tricky.

When hanging this second window piece, align the edges above the window for a neat seam, placing as much of the new piece on the wall as you can. The top corner of the molding will prevent you from laying this piece completely down on the wall. Take care to support this piece, because its weight could easily cause it to tear at the corner of the molding.

Maneuver the paper against the wall to the top corner of the molding. Feel the corner through the paper with your finger. Place a razor blade at that point, and make a slice, diagonally down into the window space. Now you can smooth the paper down the sides of the window trim.

At the bottom corner, again feel with your finger to find exactly where the corner is. Make a cut, bringing the razor blade diagonally up into the window space. Smooth the rest of the strip down to the wall now, wrapping the excess tightly around the window.

There's no real secret to getting past windows easily. You may find that although you've matched the seam at the top of the window, the pattern and seam may seem to be a bit off at the bottom, under the window. This'll happen. Sometimes it's impossible to avoid due to bulging or strangely unplumb walls. Before cutting off the excess paper, examine the seam below the window and line it up as best you can. You may have to pull or push your edge (hopefully only slightly). Just do the best you can, and move on.

For cutting around doors, the same principles apply as for cutting around windows.

STEP 9: *Make Nice, Neat Corners*

As you come to an inside corner, align and butt your seams as usual, then carefully smooth the piece into the corner. Be sensitive with the paper. You can easily puncture it here, either with your finger or your brush. Your piece may wrap into and then out of the corner neat and wrinkle-free (especially if the house is fairly new). Or it may go into the corner fine, but then crease as it comes out on the other side.

To get rid of a crease, find the point in the corner where the crease begins. Is it closer to the top or the bottom? With a sharp razor blade, make a cut in the corner at that point, and run your blade carefully down (or up) along the corner to the end of the sheet. Now you can lift the section of paper that's been "freed" and re-lay it, smoothing out the crease.

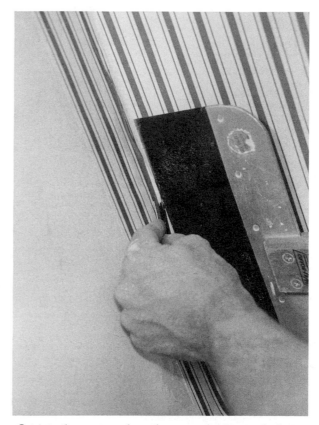

Cut into the corner, where the crease begins, to the bottom of the strip.

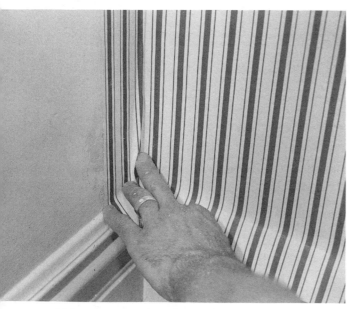

Most corners aren't perfectly plumb, which you'll see if the strip creases at some point near the top or bottom.

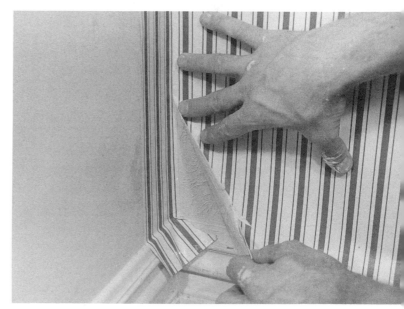

Though the pattern may be slightly interrupted at these corner points, the eye will hardly notice it later.

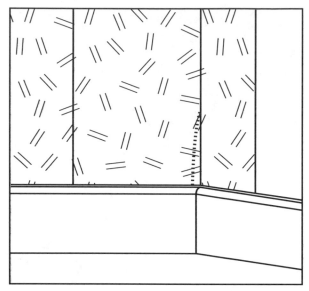

Now straighten the edge of the piece so that one flap sits under the other.

You'll notice that where you've made your cut, you have an overlap now, at the two new edges of wallpaper. Just wrap the larger one under the one that sits flushest with the corner. If you're using a vinyl, you'll want to use a little seam adhesive at this overlap, because vinyl won't really stick to vinyl without it. Apply it with a brush or with your finger, and wipe off the excess with your clean sponge.

Whether your corner piece wraps smoothly or requires a little surgery, remember to draw a new plumb line now that you're starting a new wall, before you put up a full piece on that surface. Starting at the edge of the piece that has just wrapped out of the corner, measure along the wall a distance that is the width of the paper plus a bit. Again draw a straight vertical line (plumb line) with your level. This plumb line will give you a guide for keeping your paper straight on this new wall.

When you hang the new piece plumb, you may find that there is some seam overlap between this piece and the previous one. That's OK; at least the succeeding pieces on this new wall will end up hanging straight and true. Don't worry—the over-

all appearance will register as correct and pleasing to the eye.

STEP 10: *Check Up On the Seams*

As you finish your wallpapering, walk around and check out your handiwork. If a seam has come up, try to roll it back down with the seam roller. If the glue there has dried, finger a little fresh glue in, roll the paper down, and sponge it clean.

If you were working with a vinyl covering, go back and check the areas where you were forced to overlap, like maybe in the corners or below a window. Although the overlap may appear to be holding, remember: vinyl will not stay stuck to vinyl. As insurance, lift up the edge of the overlapped strip, and use a finger (or a small artist's brush) to apply some border/seam adhesive. Then you're sure these overlapped areas won't come up later.

STEP 11: *Clean Up*

You've checked the seams and double-checked that all the adhesive is cleaned off the front of the paper. So now, clean your tools, throw away your scraps, put your furniture back, and enjoy your new room!

HANGING REGULAR (NON-PREPASTED) WALLPAPER

The methods of hanging a prepasted wallpaper are the same methods used to hang a regular wallpaper (the kind that requires you to brush glue on to the back side). With regular wallpaper, I also cut pieces in advance, just as I described doing with prepasted. The only difference is glue, so this section will mainly talk about how to apply the glue.

TOOLS AND MATERIALS

The items you need for applying regular wall coverings are pretty much the same as for prepasted papers (see the list earlier in this chapter of the tools and materials for prepasted coverings). The main difference is that now you need the glue, a bucket to mix it in (if it's in powder form), and an applicator (a big 8-inch brush or a regular 9-inch paint handle aand sleeve). And of course you don't need the water tray.

APPLYING THE GLUE

For applying the glue onto the wallpaper, you'll need a clean, flat work surface. If you've got a wallpapering table at your disposal, well, that's excellent! I own a couple of collapsible legs (sort of like inverted sawhorses) that, together with a 3-by-5-foot piece of plywood, make my table.

Wth the strip laid out on the table, roll the glue onto the back side, being careful to cover it completely.

I didn't actually have this setup for the first couple of my wallpapering years. When I first started, I would bring a new 9-by-12 sheet of plastic (1 or 2 mils thick), cover a table that was close by, and use that as my glue station. If there was no table, I would spread out the plastic on a large expanse of floor (which I'd cleaned first), tape it down taut, and use that.

If you have a flat piece of wood down in the garage—3 feet by 5 feet, or even 3 by 4, but the larger the better—that would work great on top of a table or on the floor. In this case, you would most probably want to set down an old sheet or drop cloth first, to avoid scratching the surface.

Oh, by the way, did you get glue in the powder form, or premixed? If you got premixed, then you paid more, but you don't have to mix it up. If you got the powder, it's very easy. Just follow the directions, mixing it in your clean bucket.

Glue can be applied with either a large adhesive brush or a paint handle and sleeve (roller). I've used both, and I really think the roller gives more assurance of spreading the glue evenly and not too thickly.

Now take your first cut piece of wallpaper and lay it, back side up, on your work area, with one end of the piece at either the very left or the very right of the area. Holding it down while rolling glue on may take a bit of getting used to, as the piece will want to reroll and move on the table. Apply the glue, taking care to get complete coverage. This is important, because any missed spots will translate into unglued patches up on the wall, and these will translate into bubbles in the wallpaper.

Apply the glue to as much of the piece as is laid out on your work surface. Then take the end of the piece by its corners and fold it over onto itself, glue to glue, "booking" it (remember?). Now you can slide the paper across the work surface to continue gluing the rest of the piece.

The cleaner you can keep the glue table during

the gluing process, the better. Wipe off glue that gets on any surfaces other than the back of the paper, which is the only place you want it, anyway. Excess glue on the worktable usually means glue on the face of the wallpaper, which means excess wiping of the front of the strip after it's been hung on the wall. I usually keep a spare clean sponge on the worktable specifically for that reason.

Read the directions for your paper to determine if the strips can be hung right away or if you need to wait fifteen minutes or so before hanging. Some papers require a little time to allow the glue to expand properly.

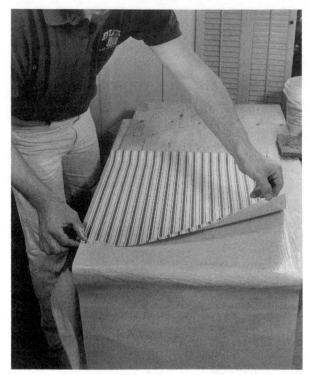

Take the end of the glued strip and fold it over onto itself (backside to backside) up to the point that the glue's been applied.

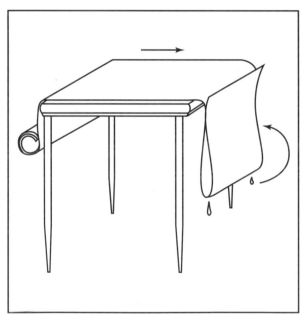

Booking the piece: After you've applied glue to the back of the strip, fold each end into the center, glue side to glue side, lining up the edges; then fold the new ends into the center again. The following photos show booking in detail.

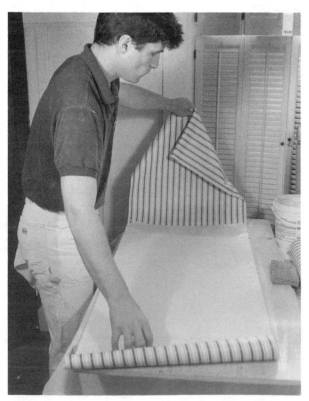

Now slide the strip down along the tabletop so that you can apply the glue to the remaining unglued back portion.

Next bring the other end of the fully glued strip up and fold it toward the center.

Bring this end to meet the other end, so that the entire piece is now glued-backside to glued-backside.

As with the pre-pasted paper, fold each side in one more time. Be careful not to crease the folds. This "books" the piece.

HANGING THE PAPER

Since the steps for hanging regular wallpaper are the same as the steps for hanging prepasted wallpaper, refer back to the step-by-step descriptions in this chapter's section on prepasted papers. Step 2 talks about the special requirements of prepasted papers, so ignore that step. Just follow Step 1 plus Steps 3 through 11 for hanging your regular wallpaper, and enjoy!

SPECIAL PAPERING PROJECTS

The art of wallpapering includes more than just basic papering of walls. Here are a couple of more specialized projects you might like to try someday.

INSTALLING A BORDER

Many wall coverings look great when finished with a border. Some patterns even come with border designs

A border can be a nice finishing touch to a room.

Recently I hung a nice flowered vinyl wallpaper in my kitchen—but I purposely ran it only halfway down the wall from the ceiling. I wanted to create the impression of a wainscoting that has a horizontal chair-rail molding. So I just used a border paper instead of actual wood molding. The border paper successfully separated the wall covering from the lower, painted half of the wall, and resulted in a really neat look.

A neighbor from my hometown named Mrs. B. G. installed a border over her wallpaper, horizontally, about a foot below the ceiling. It looked great! The point is, you can put borders anywhere you want—including in a room that has no wallpaper. Just affix the border over the paint.

To apply the border, use a border-and-seam adhesive. The stuff is strong, and smells a bit like Elmer's glue. Apply it to the back of the border with a paintbrush. The stuff dries quickly, so once the paper is in place, be sure to clean any adhesive off the front. Because you're dealing with only a few inches of wall covering, just overlap each succeeding piece (matching the pattern, of course). Then double-cut each seam where they overlap. (See the section on "Tricks of the Trade" later in this chapter for details on double-cutting.)

suggested, appearing right in those wallpaper books in the store. A border can really smarten up a job.

Borders can be put just about anywhere that strikes your fancy. Border papers can look terrific around the top of a wall, especially with a vertical stripe pattern. In this way, they serve like a decorative crown molding.

Place the glued border in position.

Overlap successive pieces and line up the pattern.

Cut through both strips at one place with your razor blade.

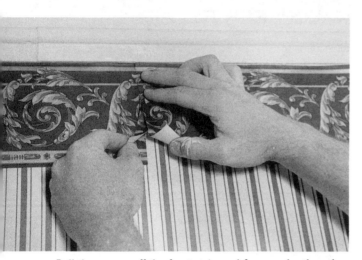

Pull the excess off the front strip and from under the other.

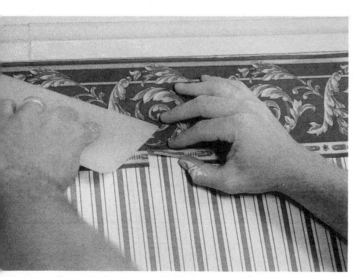

Smooth the two matched pieces together.

PAPERING A CEILING

A papered ceiling can look great! But it also can be a very difficult job. The steps to follow are pretty much the same as with wall hanging, the difference being gravity. Having a helper, each of you with a ladder, is a must.

Whenever I install paper on a ceiling, I just do the best I can with the seams. Some turn out meeting nicely, and some overlap. You may find it next to impossible to align and butt the seams as well as you've been doing on the walls.

Even with overlappings or mismatched pattern repeats, the overall effect will come across pleasingly. When I look up at a completed ceiling job, these slight imperfections seem hardly noticeable.

TRICKS OF THE TRADE

One of the enjoyable sidelights to learning a new skill is picking up the helpful tricks that professionals use to make their work easier and more attractive.

DOUBLE-CUTTING

This is a spiffy little technique that can be used to get an excellent "seamless" seam on patternless wallpapers.

Rather than fuss with aligning and butting the edges of these papers, deliberately overlap your current piece over the previous one. Let it lap over, say, an inch or so. Smooth it down as usual.

Take a straightedge (a long metal ruler) and position one edge of it directly down the middle of your overlapping seam. Holding the straightedge securely and using it as a guide, carefully run a new razor blade down the paper, starting at the very top. Your aim is to cut cleanly through both pieces of wallpaper at the overlapped seam. (Keep the razor blade in place each time you slide the straightedge down a bit, to ensure that your cut will be continuous and unbroken.)

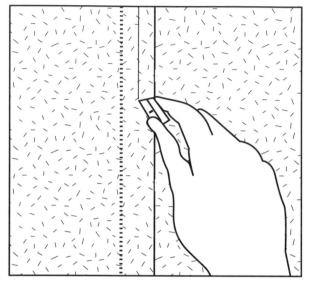

Cut through both strips along the middle of where they overlap.

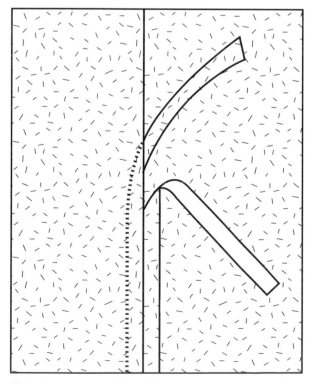

Pull the excess bits off, both from underneath and on top of the piece of wallpaper.

After you've made the cut the full length of the piece of paper, peel off the long, narrow outer strip that you've created with your cut. Then reach beneath the seam and pull out the inner strip, which also was created when you made your cut through both pieces of paper. With this excess paper out of the way, smooth the two new edges together. You'll find that they butt and lie perfectly: You have created a custom-fit seam. Remember, though, that this works only with patternless coverings. If you try to double-cut two pieces of a patterned paper, you'll throw the patten off; it won't match.

WALLPAPER REPAIR

Your job is finished, but you find one or two bubbles. Or you scratch the front of your nice wallpaper job. Here's what you can do in those cases.

Fixing Bubbles

When you find bubbles after the job is complete, try rolling them down with your seamer. While you're in the process of hanging, lots of little bubbles may come up here and there. Maybe all that's needed is to prick it with a pin. After smoothing, and a few

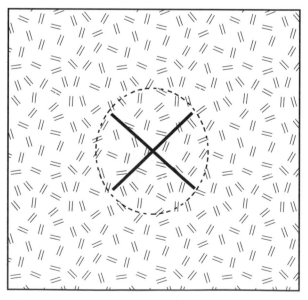

If there's a bubble showing and the wallpaper's long been dry, cut an "X" across it.

hours' time, they usually flatten themselves out. But if the bubbles are still there the next day, then possibly this is one of those dreaded dry spots, with no glue behind it.

Hopefully, it's in an inconspicuous spot. But even it it's not, take a razor blade and make an "X" cut, extending out slightly beyond the raised area. Carefully lift the edges of the paper at this cut, and stick a little wallpaper glue inside.

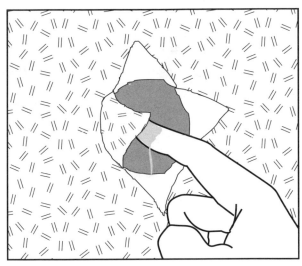

Pull back the flaps and, with a small paint brush or your finger, put some glue in.

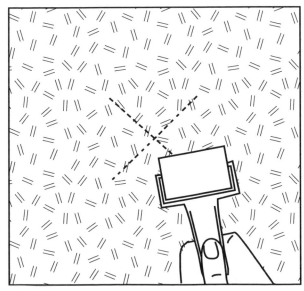

The seam roller will set the edges nicely; follow up by carefully wiping with a clean sponge.

To apply the glue, sometimes your finger will work just fine, although it could be a really small bubble, which required a really small "X." I saw in one how-to book a recommendation to use a hypodermic needle for inserting the glue. That would work (though I, myself, don't keep many of those around). Anything small will do: a popsickle stick, sliced in half; or a small artist's paintbrush.

After you get the glue inside, gingerly lay the little corners of paper back down. Roll over the area carefully with your seam roller to force out the excess glue. Lightly wipe the paper with a sponge, and you should be in great shape.

Scratches and Tears

What if you scratched or tore the front of your wall covering? Many times it's just a small portion of the front of the actual paper that's been scratched off but is still hanging there. It's easy to just take a little glue and your seamer and roll it a few times; it would then look fine.

If the damaged area is a bit bigger than this—especially if a part of the paper is actually missing—get a piece of leftover wallpaper. In the leftover piece, find the same part of the pattern to match the dam-

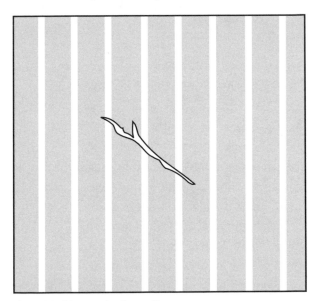

A noticeable tear in the wallpaper.

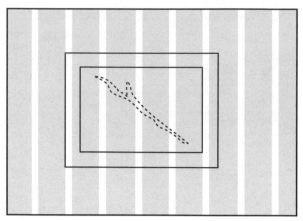

Place a small piece of wallpaper over the tear, matching up the pattern. With a razor blade double-cut a square within the patch and around the tear.

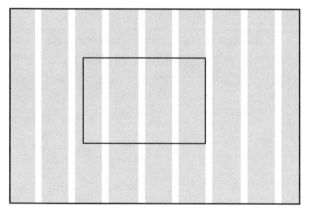

Remove the excess from around the newly cut square of the patch, as well as the torn piece underneath. Smooth down the edges of the repair.

aged section. Cut a square that's a couple of inches larger in each direction than the damaged area.

Glue the piece, and stick it to the wall over the damaged area. Be sure that the pattern on the left-over piece matches the pattern on the wall. Cut a smaller square within this larger square. Be sure to cut cleanly through the leftover piece as well as through the original wallpaper.

What you're doing is double-cutting. Pull off the excess frame of the square. Lift the square up so you can also pull out the damaged stuff. Now put the small square back on the wall to replace the damaged paper. Roll the new square with the seamer, and wipe it clean with the sponge.

DEALING WITH DARK WALLPAPER

If you selected a dark wallpaper for your job, you'll find that it's incredibly difficult to hang a completely "seamless" job. The white paper (or vinyl) backing always seems to show through, just enough, to call attention to the seams.

At the start of the job, take a swatch of your wall covering to an art supply store and pick out a water-soluble felt tip marker (not a permanent marker) in a color that matches the prominent color of the paper.

When you've finished hanging the room, check over your job. Wherever a white seam shows, color it with the marker. Let it sit for a couple of seconds, then wipe the area clean with your sponge. If the ink washes away completely, wait till that spot is dry and try again (leaving the ink on for six seconds this time). The seam should be less noticeable now.

TRIMMING THE SELVAGE

In the old days, most wallpapers were manufactured with a little extra paper on each edge, running up and down the entire length of the roll. It was called "selvage" (still is, actually). This selvage was mainly left on to protect the edges of the roll from damage. The selvage had to be trimmed off before the paper was hung.

Today, almost all papers and vinyls come pre-trimmed, with no selvage. But you may occasionally run across a paper that includes selvage, because many handprints, foils, and other expensive coverings still come with this edge.

With a patternless covering, you can leave the selvage on, overlap the pieces as you hang them, and simply double-cut the overlapped seams. (See the instructions in this chapter for double-cutting.) This will not only get rid of the selvage, but will also leave you with an excellently butted seam.

If the covering has a pattern, the selvage will have to be trimmed before gluing or hanging. This trim must be straight, because the cut is creating the edge that will be part of your permanent seam between two pieces of paper. When I come across papers with a selvage, I use a good 36-inch straightedge as a guide and cut very carefully with a razor blade.

It's almost impossible to get a perfect cut from one end of the roll to the other, but do the best you can. There will most probably be small guides printed on the edge for you to line up the straightedge on. Actually, though, if you're dealing with an expensive handprint, why are you doing it yourself? Hire a paperhanger!

WALLPAPERING AT A GLANCE

PREPARING TO WALLPAPER

MATERIALS CHECKLIST

☐ Paint scraper (6-inch blade or wider)

☐ Wallpaper sizing

☐ Paint tray

☐ Paint handle and sleeve (roller)

☐ Paintbrush

☐ Mixing bucket

☐ Drop cloths

☐ Sandpaper

☐ Stepladder

☐ Plaster (drywall compound; joint compound; Spackle)

☐ Primer

THE BASIC STEPS

1. Clear the area by moving furniture and protecting floors.

2. Paint first, by now doing any painting that is needed.

3. Repair and smooth the walls.

4. Consider "sizing" the walls.

HANGING PREPASTED WALLPAPER

MATERIALS CHECKLIST

☐ Wallpaper

☐ Putty knife (minimum 6-inch-wide blade)

☐ Smoothing brush (or smoothing knife)

☐ Two large sponges

☐ Seam roller (seamer)

☐ Border/seam adhesive (for vinyl paper)

☐ Level (or plumb bob)

☐ Tape measure

☐ Pencil

☐ Single-edge razor blades

☐ Drop cloths

☐ Stepladder

☐ Water tray

☐ Trash bag

THE BASIC STEPS

1. Draw a plumb line on the wall.

2. Activate the glue; "book" the strip.

3. Hang the first piece.

4. Smooth and sponge.

5. Trim off the excess paper.

6. Smooth the edges down.

7. Hang the next strip (and the next).

8. Cut around windows and doors.

9. Make nice, neat corners.

10. Check up on the seams.

11. Clean up.

HANGING REGULAR (NON-PREPASTED) WALLPAPER

MATERIALS CHECKLIST

Materials for hanging regular wallpaper are the same as for prepasted wallpaper, except that no water tray is needed, and the following additional items are used:

☐ Glue

☐ Bucket (for mixing glue, if it's in dry form)

☐ Glue applicator (8-inch brush or 9-inch paint handle and sleeve and paint tray)

THE BASIC STEPS

The steps in hanging regular wallpaper are the same as for prepasted wallpaper, except that glue must be applied to the paper. For hanging regular paper, follow the 11 steps for prepasted paper, but ignore step 2.

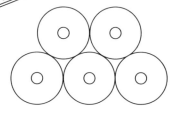

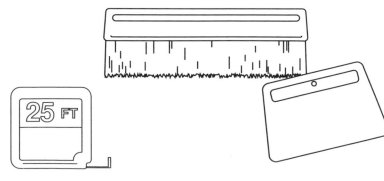

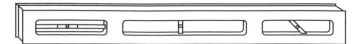

REFINISHING WOOD FLOORS

Wood flooring raises the value of any home. It adds a richness to any living area. But is yours starting to look a little scraggly? Maybe you can tell where most of the foot traffic has been because the shine has worn away. Or maybe there are more scratches than you can ignore. I mean, have you noticed that the number of throw rugs you have around the place has increased dramatically? Very possibly just touching up the finish a bit will restore your floor's wonderful luster. Then again, sanding and replacing the finish may be the way to go. On the following pages I've laid out guidelines for floorboard repair as well as the very do-able steps to take should you decide to refinish your floor yourself.

THE BASICS OF WOOD FLOORS

Wood floors come in all kinds of woods and patterns. Maple, pine (a very soft wood), and birch are used. Most common are oak floors (oak is a nice hard wood). They can be made up of simple planking, up to $3/4$-inch thick. There are herringbone patterns, inlaid borders, and parquet squares.

Most hardwood floors consist of basic plank flooring, usually $5/16$-inch-thick oak. And lengths of wood installed within the past twenty years may be interlocked, one plank with the next (called tongue-and-groove flooring).

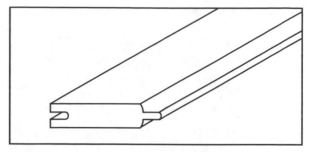

Some flooring planks are tongue-and-groove, which makes them sit snugly together when installed.

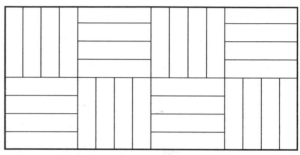

A parquet floor pattern (called a basket weave in bricklaying).

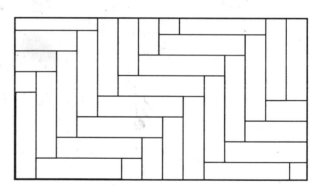

A herringbone pattern.

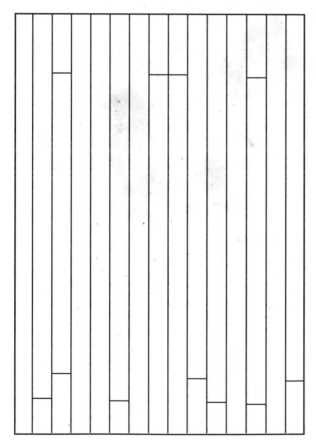

Hardwood floors that are laid out strip to strip in a simple plank pattern.

Most flooring can take four or five (or sometimes even more) sandings before there's no floor left. (Parquet panels may be able to withstand only three or four sandings, because they're usually thinner to start than typical oak planks.) A professional refinisher can sand a floor and take off only $1/32$-inch-of the wood surface. A first-timer will probably sand off a bit more: $1/16$-inch or even $1/8$-inch.

FIXING SMALL PROBLEMS

First off, it's not always necessary to sand your floors down to the new wood to get rid of minor problems. If it's merely a scratch or one small gouge that is bothering you, it can be easily fixed.

Fixing Scratches

If your floors have been finished "naturally" (that is, there was no stain involved, only polyurethane or varnish was used to seal and coat the wood) then you can simply get a small container of the material your floors were coated with. The most common floor-finishing materials—polyurethane, urethane (water-based polyurethane), and varnish—are nearly identical. If you're unsure which was used on your floors, get a small can of polyurethane. Try to match the sheen of the floors, whether it's satin, semi-gloss, gloss, or high gloss.

With a tiny brush, apply the polyurethane across any scratches. Usually a scratch through the top coat will have scratched down to the wood (that's why it shows up). So this porous part of the wood, though

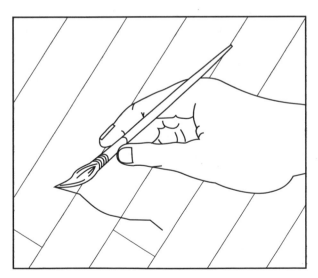

Apply polyurethane to a scratch with an artist's paintbrush.

as thin as a line, will absorb the polyurethane you've just applied. Wipe the excess polyurethane off the floor before it dries. (Bear in mind that if it does dry, it won't be greatly discernible to the naked eye, at least not straight on. It's just that from a distance, the new patch of polyurethane will show up as light reflects off the floor.) Oh, and if the floors are top-coated with wax, a little buffing with a rag should help cause the scratch to pretty much disappear.

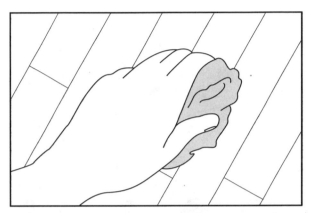

The scratch will absorb the polyurethane, so wipe off any excess around it.

If a stain was worked into your floor originally (they weren't finished naturally), then applying polyurethane to a scratch will help but won't really cause the scratch to disappear. Start by touching up the scratch with a bit of the stain color. They actually sell felt-tip furniture touch-up markers. Try and find one that's the same or similar color, and draw right over the scratch. Or you can pick up a little can of stain, again as close in color to the original as you can get. Unless it's way off, it should do fine. I mean, it's only a scratch. Rub it into the scratch. Wait for it to dry (usually overnight is a safe bet), and apply the polyurethane as described above.

Fixing Gouges

If there's an actual gouge in the floor, fill it with latex wood filler, using a putty knife to smooth it in place. After the wood filler dries, sand it and proceed to the staining (if needed) and polyurethane. A gouge repaired with wood filler always seems to be visible, so don't despair. If the gouge is in a really noticeable place in the room, you might try a stain on the wood filler (even if the floors were finished naturally) to really try and blend the patch. Or you can cover it with a rug.

An unsightly gouge in the floor can easily be filled.

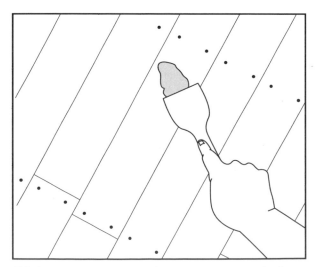

Fill deep gouges with wood filler using your putty knife.

THE VOICE OF EXPERIENCE

A Fresh Look

In some cases you can "refinish" your wood floor without machine-sanding it, by just recoating it with polyurethane. The owner of my apartment building once called me up and asked if I could do just that. He wanted me to put a fresh coat of varnish on a studio apartment's floors, without any heavy-duty sanding: just to "spruce them up a bit."

My initial reaction (privately) was, "Wow, how cheap can you get?" The floors weren't in bad shape. A bit worn and scratched, but there was no real warping or bad water damage. On my hands and knees, I hand-sanded the floors, but without using a lot of elbow grease. I did this for two reasons: to smooth down any little bumps or irregularities in the surface and to give the existing somewhat-glossy finish a tooth (that is, a dulled surface to provide a good base for a subsequent coat to adhere to).

Then, after vacuuming thoroughly for dust, debris, and dirt particles, I applied a coat of semi-gloss polyurethane with a 4-inch brush. (I could have done it with a large pad applicator, but at the time I was too lazy to go back to the hardware store to get one. The brush didn't take that much longer, since the work involved only one large room and some steps.)

I was quite surprised and impressed with the results. To be sure, the floor did not look like it had been resanded, yet the uniform sheen in the new coating gave it a fresh, clean appearance.

REFINISHING THE ENTIRE FLOOR

Well, if it's a combination of scratches, worn-away finish, discolored or warped wood, and/or if your floors have endured normal to heavy traffic for five or more years, it may be time to go all the way with sanding and refinishing.

Keep reading, and I'll show you how to refinish the floors yourself. However, if you decide to go with a professional, know that they usually charge by the square foot. This price includes sanding and finishing natural with three coats of polyurethane, or a sealer and two finish coats. Prices in New York City range anywhere from $2.00 to $3.50 a square foot, or more. Down in Miami, it could be as low as $1.50. San Francisco contractors seem to charge almost as much as New Yorkers, around $2.25 a square foot. If you live in a less metropolitan area, the price will probably be less, especially if there is healthy local competition. Also, additional finish coats may increase the price. Or if you decide to have the wood stained prior to the polyurethaning, that will make it a more expensive job.

Although the sanding machines used by professionals will be a bit more sophisticated and have more horsepower than the ones available for rent, the steps he or she takes to refinish a floor will basically be the same as those outlined for you on the following pages.

PREPARATIONS FOR SANDING AND REFINISHING

So you've decided to do the floors yourself. Now there's a few things to do to get ready for the work.

TOOLS AND MATERIALS

Following are the tools and materials needed for preparing to sand and refinish your wood floors.

- Claw hammer
- Nail set (or punch)
- Finish nails (1 1/4-inch and 1 1/2-inch)

- Chisel
- Slip-joint pliers

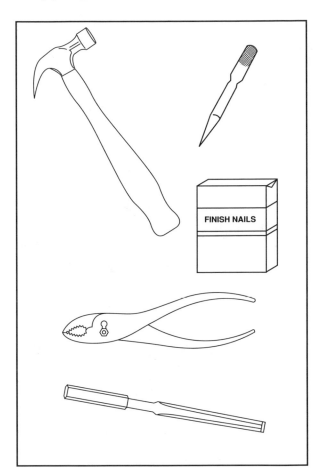

PREPARATIONS, STEP BY STEP

STEP 1: *Clear the Area*

It would probably be a good idea to get everything out of the room, now. Know that anything left in there will have a layer of sawdust after the sanding.

STEP 2: *Repair the Floorboards*

What condition are the floors in? In other words, how bad are they? With a little preliminary work at this stage, you can get the floors in good shape, ready for sanding and refinishing.

NAIL LOOSE FLOORBOARDS

Are any of the floorboards loose? If you look closely at the planks, you will see rows of nails through the boards. The nails go through the planks and sub-flooring and into the floor joists, which are the pieces of structural lumber that hold your floor up, usually at intervals of 8 inches.

The nails can eventually work loose because wood, a natural fiber, will absorb or exude moisture with changes in temperature and humidity. (Your floors are wood, or some kind of wood/glue/pulp/plywood product, and chances are that your subflooring is, too.) This is actually a lot of "activity" for a seemingly inanimate object. So these places where the floorboards are nailed through the sub-floor into the joists can become loose (floor squeaks). Take your hammer and nails and drive a nail or two in, fairly close to the others. One may do the trick, or it may take a couple of new nails to bring the floorboards back flush against the subfloor.

Or it could be a question of rotting joist, but I hope not. Only because that would be a whole-nother-ballgame in repair, and we're not going to get into infrastructure repair (at least not in this book).

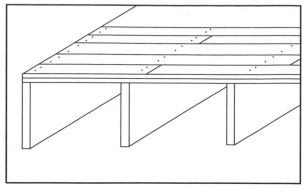

The floorboards sit on the subfloor (usually plywood), which in turn sits on the floor joists underneath.

COUNTERSINK PROTRUDING NAILS

While you've got hammer in hand, now is a great time to countersink any nails protruding from the floorboards. Even if you can just see the head of the nail, it's a good idea to pound these shiners (as they're called in the trade) back in. If they're left showing, you run the risk of tearing the sheet of paper on the sanding machine (you'll see what I'm talking about). Holding your nail set on the head of the nail, merely tap the top of it once or twice to sink the nail just under the top of the floor surface.

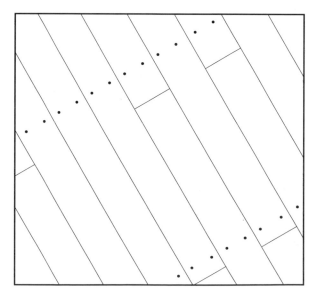

If you look carefully, you should be able to see rows of nails, usually spaced about 8 inches apart, that hold the floor planks down to the joists.

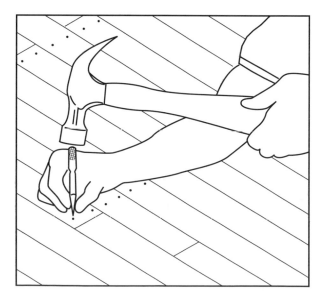

Countersink any "shiners" (protruding nails) before sanding to help avoid getting any tears on the sandpaper down the line.

ELIMINATE WATER STAINS

It seems one reason for wanting to refinish a floor is to get rid of water stains. You (or a previous tenant or home owner) may have consistently overwatered that huge ficus by the window, creating a big dark ring in the floor. Or a vase of flowers may have been knocked over by a cat when no one was around, with the water left to seep into the floor. Even more common (and beyond your control), that old steam heater against the wall leaked more than once, leaving a discolored section in the floor beneath it.

Many minimal stains can be sanded out at the same time the rest of the floor is sanded. As you work over them with the sander, you should be able to get them out, without going too far down into the wood.

Some water stains may have been absorbed pretty deeply into the floorboards. An easy trick to "eras-ing" water stains is to turn the stained floorboards over. You won't be able to do this with tongue-and-groove planks, which are interlocked and can't be pulled up without tearing the edges. But you should be able to pull up planks in most older floors, which end up having all kinds of history stained into them.

Figure which boards are involved most severely. Find the ends, and work your chisel in to lift out each board. Pull the loose nails out of the board and/or the subflooring, either with the claw of your hammer or a pair of pliers. Now just turn each plank over and renail it into the joists, through the subfloor, with 1 1/2-inch or 1 3/4-inch finish nails.

REPLACE FLOORBOARDS IF NECESSARY

On an unpleasant note: A flooring contractor just told me that urine tends to go right through to the other side of a board. So if you've pulled up the carpeting and found a smelly discolorment in the floor (dog or cat, before you moved in, to be sure), it may be just as well to go to a home improvement center and get some new planks. Obviously get planks the same width as those on your floor, saw them to length to fit, and nail in place. The sanding will bring them down to the level of the surface of the rest of the floor.

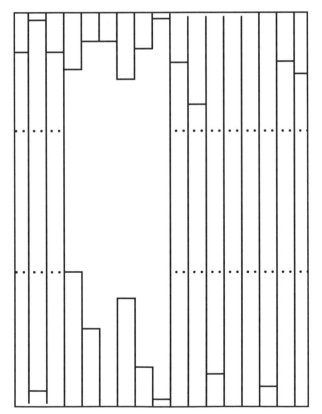

If you have a badly defined scar or water stain (and your floorboards aren't tongue-and-groove), remove the worst strips and flip them over, renailing them into the subfloor.

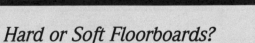

THE VOICE OF EXPERIENCE

Hard or Soft Floorboards?

Does it matter? Well, hardwood floors, like oak, will probably take four or five sandings in their lifetime before you sand off the entire board, which is usually about 5/16" thick. The sanding process is much quicker with a soft wood, like pine, and the results are apparent earlier. Realize, though, that you can easily sand through a pine floorboard if you're not paying attention (I know, I've done it).

STEP 3: *Rent the Sanding Machines*

You should be able to find everything you need at the place where you rent the sanding machines. Look in the Yellow Pages under "Floor Machines: Renting." If there are more than one, call and find out their prices. Be sure they indeed carry everything you need. Ask if it's necessary for you to reserve machines ahead of time.

THE MACHINES

You'll be renting and using two different machines. One sands the main surface of a floor; the other one takes care of the edges.

The drum sander will sand most of the room. It's the larger of the two machines, and stands about three feet high. You grip it with two hands as you guide it back forward and then back across the floor. A piece of sandpaper attached to the machine rotates and, with floor contact, sands the floor.

These machines will not be quite as powerful as the ones the professionals use. Chances are yours will sand when you turn the machine on and stop when you tilt it back. Some places, however, offer drum sanders with a lever that raises and lowers the drum. This gives you much more control and offers a smoother transition between sweeps, making it less likely that you'll cause sander lines or grooves. If they have the lever machine, get it.

The second machine you'll use is the edger. It will sand up the three-or-so-inch perimeter of the room that the belt sander can't reach. Though small, it's louder than the drum sander.

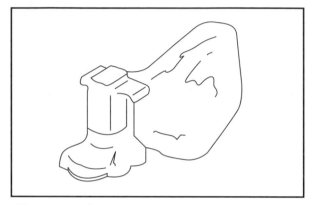

Edger

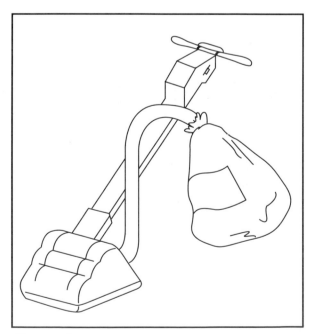

Drum sander

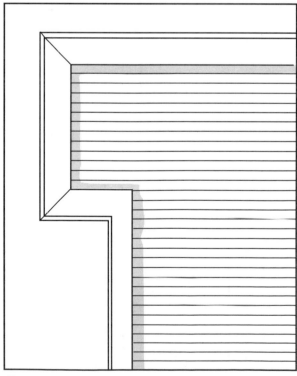

The drum sander will be able to reach most of the floor, leaving the perimeter for the edger (and the corners for the scraper).

THE SANDPAPER

You will also need paper for each of your machines. The paper for your drum sander is one long piece that wraps around the drum. The edger paper is round-shaped and called a disc. If you're sanding varnish off a floor, you can start with a rough-medium grit and then go right to a fine grit paper. But if there's a lot of wax buildup, the floors are in really bad shape, or there's a coat of paint on them, you ought to figure on having paper for three sanding stages: rough, medium, and fine.

Tell the clerk at the rental place how large the room is that you're working on and what condition the floors are in. He or she should be able to tell you how much sandpaper you might need, and what grit. Any sandpaper you don't end up using can be returned when you bring the machines back, so load yourself up with extra.

THE VOICE OF EXPERIENCE

Getting Information

At the place where you rent your floor sanding machines, they'll almost certainly load you up with information. If you have to, though, ask the clerk to show you how to put sandpaper on the machines. Find out how much paper, and what specific grit, he or she recommends for the size and condition of the floor you're working on. Also ask how much polyurethane the clerk thinks you'll need for your refinishing job. Most likely at least 80 percent of their business is to first-time users, so generally they will offer a lot of help and information whether you ask or not.

THE SCRAPER

With the drum sander and the edger, you will be able to sand the entire surface of the wood flooring. Well, almost. The only part left will be the corners.

The professionals scrape off the old finish in the corners with (you guessed it) a floor scraper. The scraper consists of a handle that holds a blade in place. By dragging it across the unsanded corner, you can scrape the old finish off, down to the bare wood. If you don't have a floor scraper or don't want to buy one, you can sand out the old finish by hand with sandpaper. This way, the corners will still be a bit raised but should look OK.

SANDING THE FLOOR

You're now ready to sand the floor down to clean wood, creating a fresh base for the coatings to follow. Put on some sneakers or rubber-sole shoes to avoid scuffing the floor once it's sanded.

TOOLS AND MATERIALS

You should look for:

- Drum sander (with a raise-and-lower lever)
- Edger sander
- Extension cords (if your power source is too far away)
- Drum sandpaper; in rough (36 grit), medium (50-60 grit), and fine (80-100 grit)
- Edger discs (sandpaper); in rough (36 grit), medium (50-60 grit), and fine (80-100 grit)
- Scraper (for corners)
- Hand sandpaper
- Dust mask or respirator
- Gloves
- Earplugs
- Plastic drop cloth

- Masking tape
- Latex wood filler
- Putty knife (6-inch-wide blade)
- Vacuum cleaner

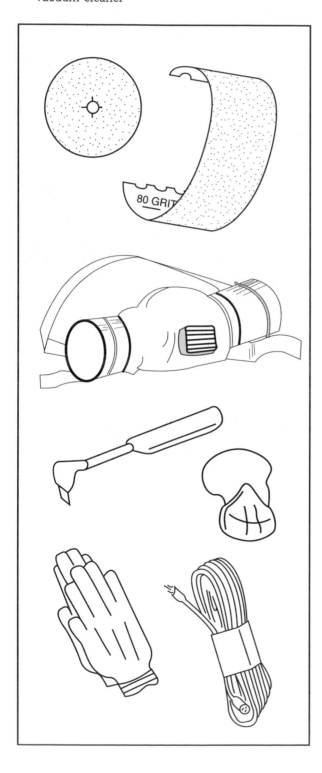

SANDING, STEP BY STEP

Though each sanding machine has its own bag that will hold most of the shavings as you go along, a lot of dust will still be raised. Unless you don't mind cleaning up the rest of the house afterward, you might want to seal off the room. For each door, cut a plastic drop cloth into a large enough piece that you can, with your masking tape, seal off the door frame. If the door closes pretty tight anyway, just stuff a towel into the space under the door, from the other side.

They probably told you at the rental place to empty the bags on the sanding machines when they get to be about half full. Wood shavings can, depending upon the type of finish that was on your floor, spontaneously combust. So keep a trash bag near your work to empty the dust into. And figure on keeping it separate from the household garbage. When the job is all finished, it would be advisable to tie the bag tightly closed and store it on concrete, away from everything else, until trash day. If you can take a drive to the dump and get rid of it as soon as you're through with the floors, even better.

STEP 1: *Rough-sand the Floor*

Load the roughest grit paper on the drum sander. Your pattern of sanding is going to be back and forth, with the grain (that is, with the floorboards). If you had hired someone to do the sanding, and your floor was relatively new (maybe eight years old), he or she might go diagonally across the grain, both ways, and then finish by going with the grain. To be safe, though, and avoid making sanding grooves, you can do a great job by just keeping your machine going with the grain.

After you plug in the power cord, sling it over your shoulder to avoid running over it with the machine (a very easy thing to do!). Set the machine upright, or lift the raise-and-lower lever, so the sandpaper is not touching the floor. Oh, and put your dust mask on and earplugs in. Now, turn the machine on.

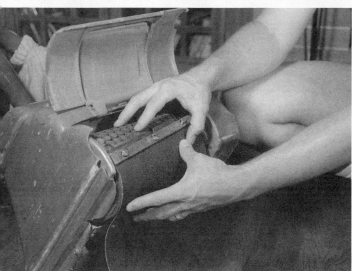

Tilt the drum sander back and install the sheet of sandpaper.

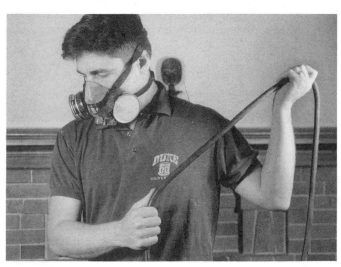

Before turning the machine on, sling the power cord over your shoulder to avoid running over it.

Start at one corner of the room. With your back to the wall, move slowly forward, guiding the machine straight along with the floorboards. Lower the drum onto the floor as you move forward. You're now sanding the finish off the floor.

As you reach the opposite wall, slowly lift the drum back up off the floor as you continue to move the machine forward. Lowering and raising the drum while the machine is moving forward or backward will help lessen sanding dips in the floor. The procedure takes a bit of careful doing, but with each pass, you will surely pick up more finesse. At this point, the machine is still on, and you are now facing the wall. Now simply repeat your motions—this time walking backward.

As you begin to move backward, again lower the belt so the paper comes in contact with the floor. Sand, sand, sand; raise the drum as you come back to your starting point, with your back again to the starting wall.

Now position yourself four or five inches farther to the left (or the right, depending on which corner you started in). It's kind of like mowing your lawn. You're ready for your second pass. Continue this routine until you've made enough passes to cover the room.

As you move forth, and then back, if you see that the finish is not almost completely coming up, don't hesitate to go again over any spots that seem stubborn. Your goal with the rough grit is to remove almost all of the old finish. Just take care to pass the machine over these spots somewhat gingerly. You want to avoid sanding a big dip in the floor.

You'll see, as you complete this first part of the process, that you're able to bring the machine for-

Using both hands, lower the drum as you walk, sanding in the direction of the floorboards.

THE VOICE OF EXPERIENCE

Blow a fuse?
Turn off the machine.

These sanding machines have a lot of power surging through them! It often happens that you'll blow a fuse or trip the circuit breaker while sanding. If you do, turn off the machine *before* you go to remedy the situation. I know it sounds pretty obvious, but listen. The power goes off, and so does your machine, but the switch is still in the "on" position. A fellow floor refinishing contractor named Teryl told me that this happened to her a few years ago. She went down into the cellar, finally found the fuse box, and replaced the fuse. As she climbed the stairs back to the room that was being sanded, she could hear the drum sander going. She raced up the stairs and found that the machine had gone along the floor to the wall, where it stopped and sanded in place—down to the subfloor!

ward and sand everything except the final four or so inches to the wall. Because of the shape of the machine, however, it will miss the final three feet or so of the floor behind you. So when you've made all your passes across the room, do an about-face and, following the same lower/raise procedure, take off that last remaining wide strip, the one that used to be behind you.

STEP 2: *Rough-sand the Edges*

Now, on to the edging, again using the roughest grit paper. The edging machine, as I mentioned earlier, though smaller than the drum sander, is a lot louder and, I think, more difficult to manage. This is the tough part and will build up your rear end and hamstring muscles. I usually get my assistant to do this part, if I can.

You never want to turn the machine on with the disc bottom sitting flat on the floor. If you do, the edger will literally take off, gouging the floor along the way before it slams into the wall.

Standing bent over, hold the machine in front of you just above the floor at the wall, and turn it on. The only way I can describe the sanding contact with

the floor is a floating motion, back and forth. You don't want to allow the edger to be sitting, with all its weight, on the floor. And yet if there's no contact between sandpaper and floor, no sanding will occur.

There's a middle ground, which calls for some balance. You kind of guide the machine back and forth, against the baseboard. You will see how quickly the edger takes up the old finish. The edger requires some skill, which you will pick up in no time.

If left too long in one place, the edger will leave circular sand grooves. But you can get them out. If you balance/float/move from side to side for a section, then finish that area up by turning the front of the edger toward the direction you're going and making one more balance/float/pass, you should be able to get rid of the sand grooves.

STEP 3: *Medium-sand the Floor*

Repeat Step 1 with the drum sander—but now use medium-grit paper. This time around, you will most certainly finish taking up all of the old finish.

STEP 4: *Medium-sand the Edges*

Now go around the perimeter of the room with the edger, using medium-grit discs. Follow the same procedure outlined in Step 2.

STEP 5: *Scrape or Sand the Corners*

Now, before starting the final passes with the finest grit paper, is a good time to scrape or sand your corners. Hold the handle of the scraper and pull the tool's blade over the corner area. You will actually scrape off the old finish down to the bare wood. Though this scraping will get the corners down farther than if you hand-sanded them, the sound is similar to fingernails on a blackboard. I, for one, happily give this step over to a coworker.

Also check for any other areas that the sanding

Guide the edger along the edge of the room, balancing it with a sort of floating motion.

machines couldn't hit, such as a wood threshold or the floor beneath a steam heater.

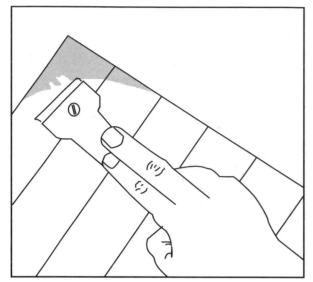

Scrape the finish off the corners with your scraper or with sandpaper.

STEP 6: *Fill Cracks and Holes with Wood Filler*

Sweep up or vacuum the excess particles and dust off the floor now. Use the latex wood filler to fill any cracks, countersunk nail holes, or gouges. With the putty knife, drag generous amounts of the material across the areas that need filling. Once filled, scrape off the excess. What you're leaving is really just a film of the stuff on the floor.

Most of the time I find myself using between half a gallon and a full gallon of latex wood filler on a job (which could be one or more rooms). I drag a film of filler across the entire floor, just to be sure I get every crack. Because the layer of filler is so thin, it should be dry in an hour or so.

STEP 7: *Fine-sand the Floor*

Make your final pass with the belt sander or drum sander, using the finest grit sandpaper.

STEP 8: *Fine-sand the Edges*

This is the final stage of sanding with the edger, this time using fine-grit sandpaper. At this point, also give the corners a final touch.

STEP 9: *Clean Up*

When you're finished sanding, wrap up the power cords. Gather up the unused sandpaper and store it and the machines somewhere, away from your newly sanded area.

If it's raining out, be careful to not let anyone walk across the floor right now. At this point, sanded down to raw wood, the floor will absorb any liquids like a sponge, and it would be very difficult to sand them out. So sealing the floor right away is the next step.

With the floor nozzle on your vacuum, carefully go over your nice bare floor now and clean up all the wood shavings. It's a good idea to give a once-over to the walls, window sills, door casings, etc., too. The point here is to vacuum up every bit of dust within your working space. You're going to be applying a wet coating to the floor. This coating will hold any particles that settle out of the air and onto the floor as it dries.

APPLYING THE FINISH

As I said, the floor ought to be sealed right away. The rental place will most probably carry polyurethane and stain, so you can pick it up now when you return the sanding machines. (Don't let anyone get on the floor now that it's clean!)

THE STAIN OPTION

Do you want to set a stain in the floors before applying the finish coating? A stain can look beautiful, to be sure. There are lots of stains: dark walnut, honey, maple, red oak, white (to mimic bleached wood).

Be warned, though: Stain is a very unforgiving sealer. Imperfections and sand lines will show up and become more pronounced, as opposed to a natural finish (urethane or polyurethane), which may actually hide uneven sanded areas. We taped an episode on wood floor refinishing for a local cable station. The contractor who was showcased advised against first-timers trying a stain.

If you're going ahead with a stain as a sealer, the basic procedure is to apply it with a brush—going with the grain and floorboards—and then wiping the excess in and off with your clean cotton rags.

Beginning at the farthest point from your exit, apply the stain with a 4-inch pure-bristle brush or applicator and pad. Usually I apply the stain all the way across the room for a width of about four or five floorboards, which is a comfortable reaching distance for me. Then I go back and wipe the excess off the surface with the cotton rags.

The longer you leave a stain on bare wood before wiping it, the darker it will become. If it takes you five or ten minutes to get all the way across the room for a width of five floorboards, that's a good amount of time to let the brushed-on stain soak in before doubling back to wipe it off. As you wipe back and forth, you're also blending and rubbing the stain into the wood.

After finishing the entire room, be sure to follow the directions on the can concerning disposal of the rags and cleaning of the brush. Most stains (except for water-based stains) include highly flammable components. Rags used for stains or for oils, such as Danish or tung, can spontaneously combust because of a high concentration of linseed oil. Usually you can clean the brush with mineral spirits (paint thinner). If you seal the oiled rags in a metal container with water in it and then drop them off at a hazardous waste site, you should be fine.

POLYURETHANE AND URETHANE

You have a choice of oil-based or water-based coatings for finishing your floors. Polyurethane is a synthetic varnish, with an oil resin. Urethane is its water-based counterproduct. But you should be aware that the oil-based polyurethanes are sometimes referred to as urethanes, while the water-based urethanes are sometimes called polyurethanes.

There are pros and cons to both variations of this product. Polyurethanes dry to a harder and more durable finish than urethanes, though innovative formulas for water-based products are catching up. Simply by putting on an additional coat of the water-based urethane on most jobs, you can pretty much match the durability of polyurethane.

And urethanes seem to be the only true "natural" finish, as they are clear and do not yellow the wood while being applied. Polyurethanes are amber colored right out of the can, and on top of that, they tend to yellow even more over time. These oil-based coatings also smell pretty bad as they cure (dry).

The most important consideration, I believe, is that although they are both chemicals, the oil-based polyurethanes are far less environmentally friendly than the water-based urethanes. By their very existence, the polyurethanes introduce a solid pollutant

THE VOICE OF EXPERIENCE

Good Enough for Pharoahs

I s varnish, or polyurethane, a lasting sealer? Archeologists have found mummy cases 2,500 years old, their surfaces still protected with the original finish. The Egyptians used the same oils (linseed, for one) as solvents for their varnishes that we use today. At museums that have ancient Egyptian exhibits, you can see the telltale pale yellow color of the varnish still intact on the pharoahs' coffins.

into the environment. And during the curing process, the oil resins release toxic elements known as volatile organic compounds (VOCs) into the atmosphere. Many states now limit the amount of VOCs emitted by products. The water-based counterparts do not emit VOCs.

Whether you go with a water-based coating (urethane) or an oil-based coating (polyurethane), you have a choice of finishes: flat (matte), satin, semi-gloss, gloss, or high gloss. The higher the sheen, the more durable the finish—though the more susceptible to scratches.

Tools and Materials

Following are the tools and materials needed for applying the finish.

- Polyurethane (oil-based) or urethane (water-based)
- Paint tray (or large shallow bucket)
- Small and large applicator pads (lamb's wool, if oil-based polyurethane) or;

  Paint brush (4-inch)
- Respirator
- Latex or rubber gloves
- Sandpaper
- Vacuum cleaner
- Paint thinner (for polyurethane cleanup)

APPLYING THE FINISH, STEP BY STEP

Set out a couple of sheets of newspaper in the room next to the one you're working in. There you can open your can of polyurethane (or urethane), stir it, and pour some into the paint tray.

Whether you chose an oil-based or a water-based coating, put on your respirator and the latex or rubber gloves. You've already vacuumed and dusted the

work area to get up every last speck of sanding dust, so the wood floor is now ready for coating.

STEP 1: *Coat the Edges*

This part of the job goes very quickly. Use the brush or small applicator pad to apply the polyurethane or urethane around the perimeter of the room. You only need to cover the first couple inches of floor out from the wall, four inches at the most.

STEP 2: *Coat the Floor*

Next, coat the rest of the floor, using either the brush or the larger applicator pad and the paint tray, always going with the grain of the wood. Start at the farthest area from your exit. (Remember the classic story of the guy who painted himself into a corner?)

STEP 3: *Lightly Hand-sand*

As each coat of finish dries, tiny bubbles may appear; small bits of dirt or dust may have been caught in the surface. It's always good practice to lightly hand-sand between coats, although it's not necessary after the first coat of an oil-based polyurethane. But with water-based urethanes, sanding at this point is a must because the initial coat will raise the grain of the wood. Some professionals use steel wool for this sanding step, but only on polyurethane. Be careful not to use steel wool on urethanes, as it will leave little fibers in the finish, fibers that will rust.

Run your vacuum cleaner over the floorboards after sanding to be sure you don't end up sealing in any little specks of dust or dirt with the next coat.

STEP 4: *Apply a Second Coat*

You should be able to apply the second coat within a few hours of the first (depending on the humidity), regardless of whether you're using a water-based or an oil-based product. Just as you did with the first

Using a brush or applicator, spread the polyurethane evenly over the floor, starting with the edges.

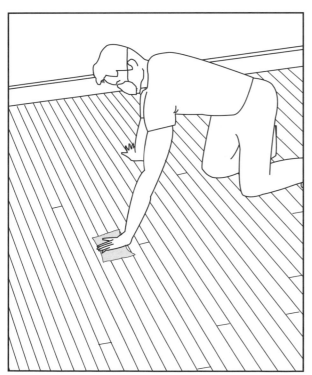

Give the dried surface a light sanding between coats to get rid of bubbles and dust particles that may have settled in the finish. Follow up by re-vacuuming.

coat, do the edges first and follow by coating the rest of the floor.

THE VOICE OF EXPERIENCE

Is a Respirator Worth the Expense?

Professionals wear respirators when they sand and when they apply the finish coat to a floor, whether it's polyurethane or water-based urethane. It makes sense. I mean, they do this kind of work every day, so they have to protect their lungs. For a one-time deal, though, it may not be worth the expense. At least wear a dust mask for the sanding part, and leave the room right after you apply each finish coat. If you do decide to purchase a respirator, a good one fitted with the proper cartridges (to filter out the bad fumes), will run you about $25 or so. If you or someone you know has one that's been sitting around the garage for a while, you'll probably want to get replacement cartridges, as they tend to loose their absorbent barrier after a few months of exposure to air.

STEP 5: *Lightly Hand-sand*

Give the floorboards a very light once-over with sandpaper. Vacuum the floor.

STEP 6: *Apply a Third Coat*

You will most certainly have to wait at least six hours, maybe overnight, before applying the third coat. Three coats of an oil-based polyurethane is a good standard for a durable floor. Even a fourth coat wouldn't hurt, especially if you spread your finish pretty thin.

As I mentioned earlier, if you're using a water-based urethane, you can be assured of matching oil-based coatings in hardness and durability by applying an additional coat (that is, four or even five coats).

Before putting the furniture back after the final coat, read the directions on drying time for the specific product you decided to go with. Water-based urethanes can take light traffic after a day, and normal to heavy traffic after forty-eight hours, under normal humidity. Oil-based coatings usually take a little longer, though there are quick-dry products on the market that can take normal traffic within twenty-four hours.

STEP 7: *Clean Up*

If you used an oil-based polyurethane, you can clean out the brush and applicator pads with mineral spirits (paint thinner). Tools for a water-based product can be cleaned with soap and warm water.

THE VOICE OF EXPERIENCE

Shellac, By Any Other Name, Is Just a Bug.

A little insect called *laccifera,* or just plain lac bug, secretes a resinous substance that protects its eggs. Unfortunately for the lac bug, people discovered that, when dissolved in alcohol, this substance forms an excellent stain killer known as (yes, you guessed it) shellac. Though today there are synthetically made shellacs on the market, most still consist of this natural secretion, which is harvested as a component.

REFINISHING WOOD FLOORS AT A GLANCE

PREPARING TO SAND AND REFINISH

MATERIALS CHECKLIST

- ☐ Claw hammer
- ☐ Nail set (or punch)
- ☐ Finish nails (1¼-inch and 1½-inch)
- ☐ Chisel
- ☐ Slip-joint pliers

THE BASIC STEPS

1. Clear the area by removing all furniture from the room.

2. Repair the floorboards by nailing loose boards, countersinking protruding nails, and turning over or replacing stained boards.

3. Rent the sanding machines and get sandpaper.

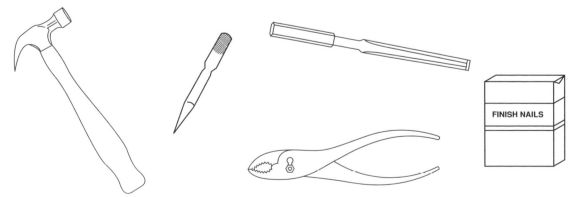

FINISH NAILS

SANDING

MATERIALS CHECKLIST

- ☐ Drum sander (with a raise-and-lower lever)
- ☐ Edger sander
- ☐ Extension cords (if your power source is too far away)
- ☐ Belt sandpaper; in rough (36 grit), medium (50-60 grit), and fine (80-100 grit)
- ☐ Edger discs (sandpaper); in rough (36 grit), medium (50-60 grit), and fine (80-100 grit)
- ☐ Scraper (for corners)
- ☐ Hand sandpaper
- ☐ Dust mask
- ☐ Earplugs
- ☐ Plastic drop cloth
- ☐ Masking tape
- ☐ Latex wood filler
- ☐ Putty knife (6-inch-wide blade)
- ☐ Vacuum cleaner

THE BASIC STEPS

1. Rough-sand the floor with the belt sander, using the roughest-grit paper.

2. Rough-sand the edges with the edger, using the roughest-grit paper.

3. Medium-sand the floor with the belt sander (medium-grit paper).

4. Medium-sand the edges (medium-grit paper).

5. Scrape or sand the corners.

6. Fill cracks and nail holes with wood filler.

7. Fine-sand the floor (fine-grit paper).

8. Fine-sand the edges (fine-grit paper).

9. Clean up by vacuuming the floor and vacuuming or dusting the walls, window sills, and other surfaces.

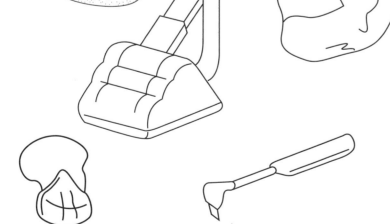

APPLYING THE FINISH

MATERIALS CHECKLIST

☐ Polyurethane (oil-based) or urethane (water-based)

☐ Paint tray (or large shallow bucket)

☐ Small and large applicator pads (lamb's wool, if oil-based polyurethane) or;

Paint brush (4-inch)

☐ Respirator

☐ Latex or rubber gloves

☐ Sandpaper

☐ Vacuum cleaner

☐ Paint thinner (for polyurethane cleanup)

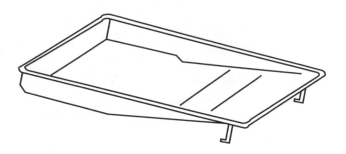

THE BASIC STEPS

1. Coat the edges.

2. Coat the rest of the floor.

3. Lightly hand-sand the floor, then vacuum.

4. Apply a second coat.

5. Lightly hand-sand and vacuum.

6. Apply a third coat (and a fourth, if desired).

7. Clean up.

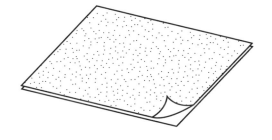

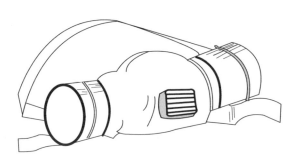

FINISHING TOUCHES

I t always amazes me to see just how easily a room can be transformed, or neatened up, with little skill or finances. Often I come across a kitchen that the owner can't afford to renovate. Replacing cabinets can make this room the most costly one in the house, but it's generally the cabinets that make the statement for the room. Within the past few years, companies have sprung up that specialize in replacing solely the doors (leaving the cabinet housing intact). This is a great money-saver compared with replacing the entire cabinet, which was the only choice one had in the past.

But what if you can't afford to do even that, which still isn't really that cheap? You can change the knobs or handles! Replacing your kitchen cabinet knobs or handles is one example of how you can spruce up a room by devoting time to details.

Details! Those little, seemingly insignificant things that can really detract from the whole picture. They may not be especially noticeable, yet attention to them can really bring it all together. There are so many ways, it seems, that we all, in our way, can pay attention to our own details; we can add our own touches to our surroundings.

These important finishing touches are what this chapter is all about. I'll look at some of the smaller projects that can make a big difference in your house. You might be surprised to see how new a room looks just by replacing cabinet handles or changing the plates over light switches or cleaning old paint off windows. We'll also get into one of the most satisfying and inexpensive ways to bring your kitchen cabinets back to life, simply painting them.

REPLACING KITCHEN CABINET HANDLES OR KNOBS

It may be that the handles or knobs you have are not in your taste, or maybe you've just grown tired of them. Could be you've seen some antique brass handles that you really like. Or your doors don't have any handles or knobs at all, and you'd like to change the look of the cabinets by putting some in. Well, the most you would need for even the biggest change in cabinet handles are the following.

- New knobs (or handles)
- Screwdrivers (Phillips and regular)
- Drill and bits
- Torpedo level
- Spackling putty
- Putty knife (2-inch-wide blade)
- Sandpaper
- Ruler

If you are merely replacing old knobs with new knobs, all you need is a screwdriver and the new knobs. Likewise if you have found new handles to replace the old ones check the spacing between the two connections on the handles. It's probably 3 inches, but it could be 3 1/4 or even 4 inches. Be sure to bring an old handle with you to the hardware store when you look for new ones. If the spacing on the connections is the same, you should be able to just unscrew the old handles and screw in the new ones.

But perhaps the doors are plain, with no pull fixtures on them at all, and you'd like to put some on. For that you will just need a drill and screwdriver, and I'll go into details of the installation a little further on in this section.

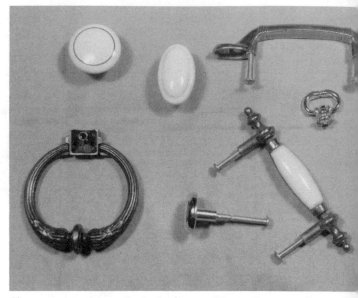

If you want to change the look of your cabinets, there are all kinds of knobs and handles out there.

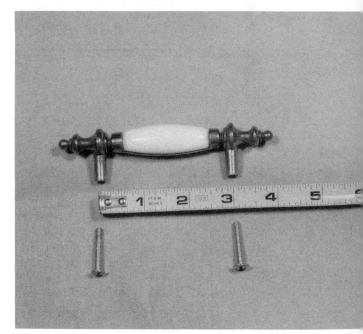

Check the spacing between the connections on your handles.

88

Perhaps you would like to switch from knobs to handles, or vice versa. Maybe you've got some ugly knobs on the doors now, and you've seen some beautiful antique brass handles you would love to put on. Chances are that you can use the single knob hole for one of the handle's two holes—or perhaps you'll need two new holes.

In case there are handles now on the doors, and you've seen some great porcelain knobs you'd like to put in, the replacement job is going to leave you with a few extra holes where the handles used to be. The simple solution is to fill the old holes, and drill new ones. (If your situation calls for you to fill holes, then you will also have to paint the fronts of the doors, and you'll find all the details on repainting later in this chapter.)

First remove the old knobs or handles. Often after a fixture has been in place for a long time in a piece of particle board that's covered by veneer (which is, by the way, what most kitchen cabinets are made of), the veneer will be raised a bit around the hole. If you find this to be the case, sand the raised area down as best you can. The point is to make the surface flat again so that after the paint and the new fixtures are in place, no one will be able to tell that anything's been changed.

If you end up with extra holes, fill them with spackling putty, using the 2-inch putty knife. Let the putty dry, then sand the patches. Chances are you'll have to repeat this step, because the putty usually shrinks as it dries.

Now hold the new knob or handle in place on one of the doors. Where exactly would you like to see it? Maybe a little higher or to the left of the old one? Now that the old holes are filled, you can put the new ones wherever you desire. Draw a little "X"

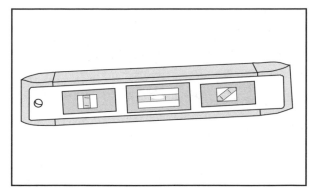

Torpedo level

as your lead where to drill the hole, and with your ruler, duplicate the location of the "X" on each door. If you're putting in handles, use your torpedo level, holding it vertically, to be sure that the location of the two holes are plumb, one on top of the other.

On the faces of drawers, no doubt you will want your pull fixture centered. Find the center with your ruler. If it's a handle (rather than a knob) that's going on, again use your level, this time holding it horizontally, to be sure that the two holes for the handle are level.

When you're ready to drill the holes, find a bit that's just a little larger than the screws that will go through the cabinet and into the fixture. (The screw will tighten once it's threaded into the back side of the knob or handle, so you don't need the added labor of having to thread it through the cabinet doors, too.) Sometimes, if you drill too eagerly, the bit will pull a small part of the veneer away with the hole as it comes out the other side. So drill through from the front to the back of each door. Then if the bit rips off a part of the surface wood or veneer, this will happen inside the cabinet and not on the front surface where it can be seen.

PAINTING THE KITCHEN CABINETS

Do you find yourself stuck with those dark-brown, fake-wood-veneer cabinets (which can look nice, but usually don't)? Well, you can do something about it. You can paint them.

Yes, you can paint them! Honestly, almost any kitchen cabinet can be painted, and this will change the look of the kitchen completely. One whole episode of our public access television show, "The Power of Positive Painting," was devoted to painting some ugly fake-wood cabinets, and we received more calls of interest for that episode than for any other. Do you have those kinds of cabinets? You know, the kind that has a sort of Western look, with a bit of Medieval mixed in? Maybe with black iron hinges?

First off, I must point out that I'm not talking about going to the trouble of painting the insides of your cabinets. To empty them out and paint them is, I feel, a complete waste of time, paint, and energy. They're only open when you open them, right? So what does it matter if they remain dark-looking inside? I am talking about painting the exterior of your kitchen cabinets: the housing and both sides of the doors. (Most of my clients also like me to paint the inside edge of all the cabinet openings.) The idea here is to lighten them up—to get rid of that dark look.

In the past, if kitchen cabinets were painted, the finish would wear or scratch off quickly because of all the handling the doors and drawers must take. Painting wasn't really an option because paints of yesteryear did not adhere well enough to the glossy (and sometimes greasy) veneers that so many cabinets have.

Today, though, by using the proper materials and following some specific, simple steps, you can paint your cabinets and have the paint job last. There are now excellent primers and finish paints on the market that will hold up under lots of hand traffic.

In a nutshell, all you have to do is clean and lightly sand the cabinet surfaces, prime them, and paint. And though these steps are simple, each one is equally important: without one being followed, you may give up the desired result of new-looking cabinets with a surface that won't scratch off.

TOOLS AND MATERIALS

Good quality, good quality, GOOD QUALITY! Often in painting, it isn't necessary to get the best or most expensive whatever; sometimes you can do just as good a job with a cheap brush, for instance. But with cabinets, a key to making sure the new finish turns out durable, and looking super, is to use only good-quality materials.

For a primer, the best way to go would be an alkyd-based product, or even an alcohol-based one (shellac). There are, however, some really high-quality water-based primer/sealers on the market. They don't smell nearly as bad as alkyds when you're applying them (I rarely use shellacs anymore, because of just that).

Painting an alkyd (oil-based) finish paint over a latex (water-based) primer could be a problem if you don't allow the first coat to cure (dry) properly first. Because each product consists of different chemical components (latex cures as the water evaporates; the alkyd dries as the resins oxidize, thus hardening), each has a different drying time. But if allowed to dry for the proper time, a latex primer will be an ideal surface for an alkyd paint. I'm suggesting that you use an alkyd for the finish coats because a very good-quality, high-resin, industrial alkyd paint will adhere to a surface better than a latex product will.

In the case of latex primers, price is actually a good gauge of quality. In other words, if the product states that it is a primer/sealer and it costs upwards of $30, then you've probably got yourself a winner, at least as far as its quality.

For alkyd-based primer or paint, choose a pure

bristle (natural fiber) brush and mohair or lamb's wool roller sleeves (with a very tight nap, about a quarter-inch). If you've decided on going with a latex primer, use a good-quality synthetic (such as polyester) brush. Even with latex, I'd suggest using mohair or lamb's wool roller sleeves.

Again, good quality is key to selection of paint. There are all kinds of paint products out there. If you're going to finish with an alkyd that was formulated for industrial use, you'll be assured of the best possible surface, one that will hold up under all the washing, scratching, and fingerprinting it will be subjected to.

How much primer and paint will you need? Enough for the cabinet doors (inside and out) and the exterior of the cabinet housing. You will most probably want to apply one coat of primer and two coats of the finish paint. In most kitchens, this translates to a quart of primer (maybe a little more) and somewhat more than half a gallon of paint. Since paint is sold in quarts, gallons, and five-gallon containers, buy two quarts of primer and one gallon of paint. If you end up needing only a single quart of primer, you can return the other one to the store for a refund.

Here is a list of the materials you need for painting the cabinets.

- TSP cleaning solution (trisodium phosphate)
- Sponge
- Bucket
- Sandpaper
- Clean rag
- Good-quality primer/sealer (water-based or alkyd-based)
- Good-quality industrial alkyd-based finish paint (with a sheen, like satin, semi-gloss, or gloss)
- Good-quality brush (2-inch or 2 1/2-inch)
- Paint tray
- Two roller tray liners

- Roller handle
- Two mohair or lamb's wool paint sleeves (with 1/4-inch nap)
- Mineral spirits (paint thinner)
- Empty coffee can

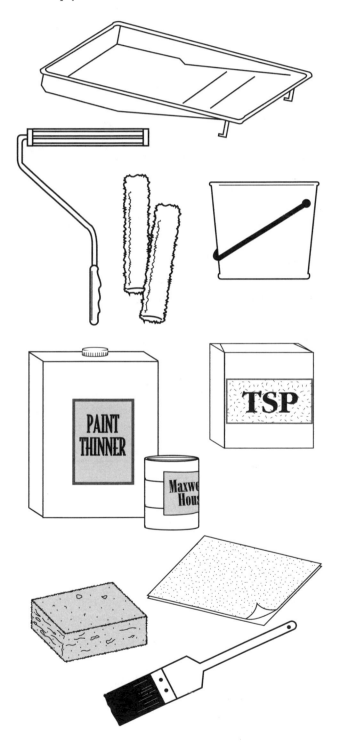

PLAN WHEN TO DO IT

Probably the day of a big dinner at your house wouldn't be a good time to paint the kitchen cabinets. The coats will dry quickly, but give yourself a three-day work span, at the very least. Figure on the first day to put on the primer, the second day for the first coat of finish paint, and the third day for putting on the final coat of finish paint.

I can't say how fast or slow each phase might take someone. Working efficiently (and having painted cabinets a few times), I can apply each coat in most kitchens in two to three hours. Most of the time I like to enjoy myself and take my time, so four hours isn't unheard of, either.

Because you're going to have some smelly paint fumes, it would be best to plan your job for a time when you can keep the windows open for ventilation (you know, a nice day).

PAINTING THE CABINETS, STEP BY STEP

STEP 1: *Remove the Hardware*

Remove handles or knobs, and any magnets. If you plan to reuse the hardware, put it and all the screws into a Ziploc bag. Lay newspaper down on the countertops and beneath the floor cabinets to serve as drop cloths.

STEP 2: *Clean the Surfaces*

First step toward creating a really good bond between the veneer (or wood) and the primer is to clean the surfaces. TSP (trisodium phosphate) is an ideal cleaner of grease and dirt. Most painters use this as their initial prep step, before priming.

TSP comes in powder form, and you can create various strengths depending on the proportion of water you mix with it. Used with a bucket and sponge, TSP is an inexpensive and effective way to rid surfaces of dirty buildup that would otherwise inhibit a good bond for the fresh coat of paint.

STEP 3: *Sand the Surfaces*

Wait until the cabinets are dry after being cleaned, and then give the surfaces a once-over with sandpaper. You really don't need to expend a lot of energy on this step. Your main objective is to dull the glossy surfaces, giving them a bit of a "tooth," which will help the paint adhere.

STEP 4: *Apply the Primer*

Whether they're real wood or fake, veneer or varnished, the cabinets must be pre-coated, or primed, before painting. By priming you will be neutralizing "hot spots"—like knots or cross-grains—thus giving the surface an even porousness for the finish paint.

Give yourself plenty of space. Clear off the counters, if there are cabinets hung above them, and the floor around your working space. Take the drawers out and put them on the counters. This way it'll be easier to paint the cabinet housing they fit into. To make the job easier, we'll be painting the cabinet doors while they remain on their hinges. And we'll paint the hinges right along with the doors, giving them a nice light look, too. You'll have to decide whether you want to paint the undersides of the upper wall cabinets.

I use both a roller and a brush for applying the primer and the paint. You aren't painting a flat wall, so the application of paint with the roller on these small surfaces may take some getting used to. The roller will be able to cover the fronts and backs, and maybe the sides, of the cabinet doors, and perhaps even the front of the cabinet housing. To tell you the truth, I use the roller to save time mostly. If you would prefer to apply the primer and paint solely with a brush, then by all means, do.

If you are using a paint roller, use it before the brushwork. As you roll on the primer, you'll find out

Leave the Doors on the Hinges

My approach to painting cabinets is to just leave the doors on their hinges while you paint. And I paint the hinges, right along with the doors.

There are a couple reasons why I like this approach. Because we're trying to change the look of dark cabinets by making them lighter in color, I like the idea of "whitening" out the hinges, which are no doubt a dark color.

And secondly, I'm lazy. Well, really: taking the doors off their hinges and painting both sides would take twice as long. And you'd need a large, clean area to be able to place the doors as you paint them—a place that's free of floating dust, which is pretty darned hard to come by. You would have to lay each door down flat to paint one side and the edges. Once that side dries, you would have to turn each door over in order to paint the other side.

So it's easier—and I think will give a better-looking job—if you just leave the doors on the hinges, right where they are, while you paint them.

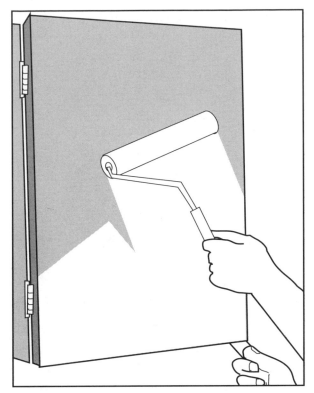

Roll the front and back of the cabinet door, holding it open with the tip of your finger.

what surfaces you can't get at and that will therefore require the brush. You'll also be able to spot any drips left by the roller and get them with the brush. Work with just a little primer on the roller, to avoid sagging of the paint coat and excessive drips. You'll find it easier that way.

As you prime the door fronts and backs, avoid allowing the doors to close all the way. Actually, if you can avoid closing any of the doors completely until after the final coat of paint has cured, you'll have a better finished job, with less chance of doors sticking to the cabinet housing. Getting the priming and painting done completely without letting the doors close, even once, may prove exasperating. But

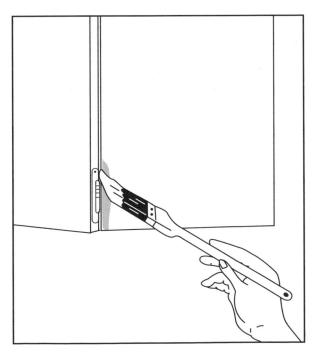

Follow up with the brushwork on the remaining areas that you couldn't get at with the roller.

you should be able to hold each door open, as you paint, with the tip of a finger at top, bottom, or edge, depending on the design of the doors.

Once the primer is rolled on every place you can roll, follow with the brush to completely prime the surfaces. Let the primed cabinets dry overnight.

If you primed with an alkyd-based product, clean-up is with mineral spirits (paint thinner). If you used a latex primer, either throw away the roller sleeve or secure it snugly in plastic with masking tape and label it for possible later use. Clean out the paint handle and brush with dishwashing soap and warm water.

STEP 5: *Apply the First Coat of Paint*

Follow the same steps for the first coat of paint as you did with the primer. (Now, since you're definitely working with an oil-based paint, allow for ventilation by opening a window.) Roll on what you can roll on, without loading up the roller with too much paint, and then brush in the rest of the surfaces.

Priming the cabinets may have given you some kind of rhythm for the work. Perhaps you found it easier, say, because of the small area, to do the upper cabinets first, left to right. You've probably also figured out by this time just where you can hold each door, as you paint it, without letting it close.

At the completion of this first coat of finish paint, figure on twenty-four hours drying time before you come back for the second (and final) coat.

STEP 6: *Do an Interim Cleanup*

Brush the excess paint in the tray back into the paint can. Into a coffee can or jar, pour a few inches of mineral spirits, just enough to cover the bristles of the brush you're about to put in it. It's generally not a good idea to leave a brush sitting in paint thinner for long periods of time, but overnight is OK.

Put the roller handle and sleeve into a small, clean plastic bag, pulling the handle off as you roll

the paint-covered sleeve up, nice and airtight, where it can stay until you need it again the next day. (Be careful of the ink on some grocery store plastic bags, which will come off on your paint.) Wipe the handle off, close the paint can, and set your stuff aside.

STEP 7: *Sand the Surfaces*

It's the next day. Run your hands across the fronts of the doors. How do they feel? Chances are they'll be smooth, but with a little bump or nib dried into the paint here and there. Now run your fine sandpaper over the painted surfaces, lightly.

You need to use even less effort than you did originally when giving the veneer a "tooth." You'll see how easily the sandpaper will smooth down the little specks and bumps that may have dried with your first coat of paint. At this point, the primer and first coat of paint are still soft (dry to the touch, but not really cured completely), so don't get too rough with the sanding or you're likely to take off the new finish.

STEP 8: *Apply the Final Coat*

You've already primed the cabinets and painted them once, so you should have a pretty good idea what areas the roller can handle and what areas need to be brushed. For this final time around, start with the brush instead of starting with the roller. If it seemed cumbersome rolling the fronts of the cabinet housing, brush this second coat on there. This time, try to cover every area with the brush, except for the front and back flat surfaces of the doors.

When you've finished the brushwork, use the roller to paint these front and back flat surfaces. The reason I usually try to finish this way is that chances are the paint will have a sheen to it. It could be a satin finish, or even a gloss. When it's dry, you want the surface to reflect light evenly, and you don't want to see brush marks. By rolling the flat surface, especially the fronts of the doors, you're assured of an even surface.

Remember, because there is a sheen involved (as opposed to a flat finish), touch-up work on areas that have already begun to dry will show up when seen from certain angles, as the light reflects off it. This is especially so of surfaces like the fronts or backs of the doors.

Anyhow, after you've finished with this final coat, leave the doors open a few inches and allow the paint to dry for about twenty-four hours.

STEP 9: *Clean Up*

So you still have that can of mineral spirits that the brush soaked in last night? Rinse the brush out in this container again, working loose most of the paint on the bristles and diluting it. If you have a wire brush, work the stubborn paint out of the bristles (away from the ferrule). Now you need another container, a clean one. Put some clean mineral spirits in there, and rinse the brush in this. The brush should come out pretty clean. You may want to take it one more step by pouring this second batch into the original container and rinsing the brush once more with clean mineral spirits. Shake the excess out.

In California you can't dump mineral spirits down the drain. It really does get into the drinking water, and I believe other states are following suit. (My sister told me that paint thinner is considered a hazardous waste where she lives in New Hampshire, and that it's unlawful to put it down the sink there, too.) Save the container of mineral spirits and find out where your local hazardous waste site is. I usually wait until I've got a lot of stuff (paint and lots unusable thinner) before I make a trip.

Take the sleeve off the roller handle, and toss it. Wipe the handle clean with a rag and mineral spirits.

STEP 10: *Do the Final Touch-ups*

If everything went well, the cabinet doors have remained open at least a little bit throughout all this. After the final coat has dried for about twenty-four hours, close the doors. The outside of the hinges may not be covered completely with paint. There may even be some drips and lumpy dried paint on them. Clean up the hinges with sandpaper, and then touch them up with the brush and some more paint.

This is also a good time to touch up any other areas that might still show a bit of dark color (where the primer and two coats of paint didn't quite cover the old, dark veneer). And, voila!

STEP 11: *Let It Cure*

If you used a high-quality industrial paint, chances are it will be completely cured within a few days. An oil-based paint may take several weeks (curing, remember, takes a lot longer than drying). Either way, be careful during this curing time: the surface will be susceptible to scratches then. Once cured, the new surface on your cabinets should hold up well to all the hand traffic it will get.

PAINTING KITCHEN CABINETS AT A GLANCE

MATERIALS CHECKLIST

☐ TSP cleaning solution (trisodium phosphate)

☐ Sponge

☐ Bucket

☐ Sandpaper

☐ Clean rag

☐ Good-quality primer/sealer (water-based or alkyd-based)

☐ Good-quality industrial alkyd-based finish paint (with a sheen, like satin, semi-gloss, or gloss)

☐ Good-quality brush (2-inch or 2$\frac{1}{2}$-inch)

☐ Paint tray

☐ Two roller tray liners

☐ Roller handle

☐ Two mohair or lamb's wool paint sleeves (with $\frac{1}{4}$-inch nap)

☐ Mineral spirits (paint thinner)

☐ Empty coffee can

THE BASIC STEPS

1. Remove the hardware.

2. Clean the cabinet surfaces with TSP.

3. Sandpaper the surfaces lightly.

4. Apply the primer (then let it dry overnight).

5. Apply the first coat of paint (then let it dry for twenty-four hours).

6. Do an interim clean-up.

7. Sand the surfaces.

8. Apply the final coat.

9. Clean up.

10. Do the final touch-ups.

11. Let it cure.

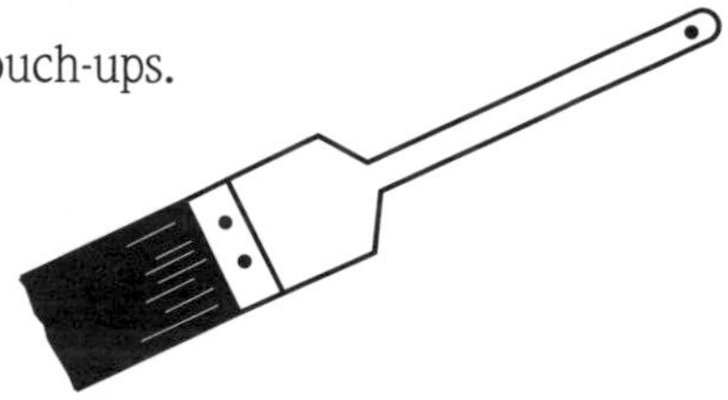

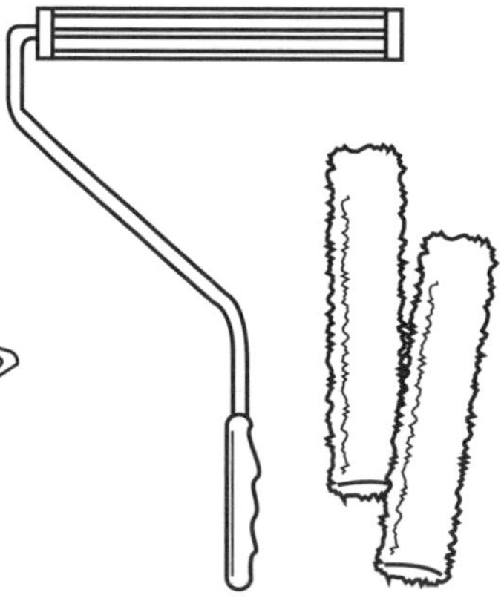

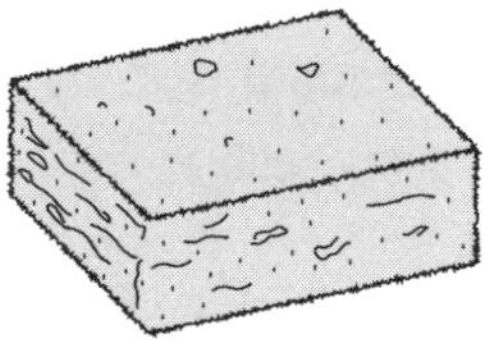

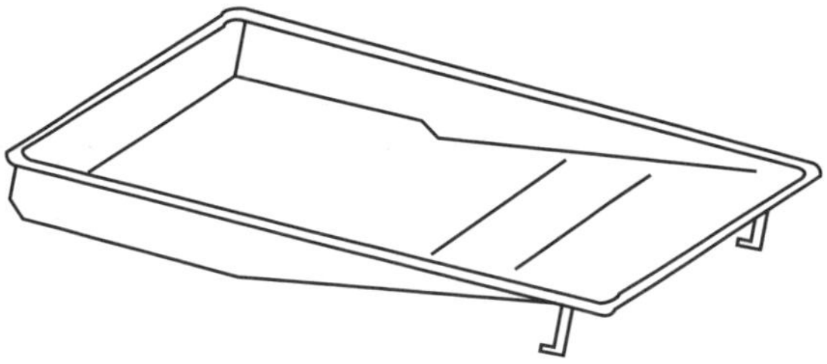

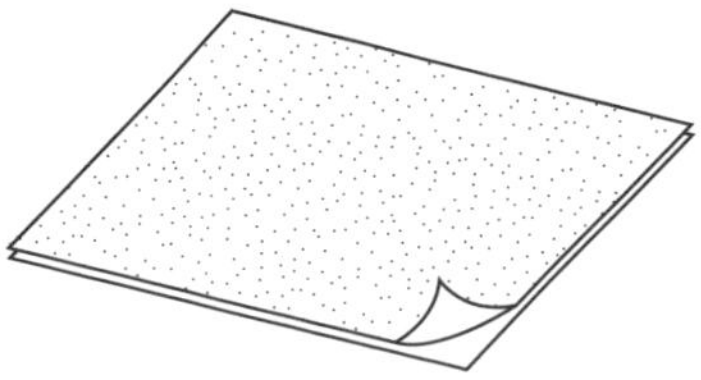

STRIPPING OLD PAINT FROM WINDOW GLASS AND DOOR HARDWARE

No matter how good a paint job is, there will almost always be a bit of paint left here and there, sometimes in highly visible spots like window glass or doorknobs. A skilled painter almost always follows up the painting with some final clean-up. It's not a bad idea to do the same thing right now, even if it's been years since the painting was done.

WINDOW GLASS

Carrying a couple of single-edge razor blades, walk through your place and look at the window panes and French doors. You may find quite a bit of paint on them. Or perhaps just a slight amount where the framing meets the glass. Simply scrape it off with the razor blades. Once scraped off, even in small amounts, your windows will look brighter and cleaner (oh, and follow up with some Windex).

DOOR HARDWARE

While walking around, you may also notice paint on the doorknobs or other door hardware. If the doorknobs weren't removed the last time the doors were painted, the rosettes may have gotten covered, and there may be paint drips on the knobs themselves. What about the strike plates and hinges?

The following is what you need for stripping old paint from door hardware.

- Paint remover
- Small pure-bristle brush
- Rubber gloves
- Steel wool (medium or fine)

Scrape old paint from window panes with a single-edge razor blade.

- Screwdriver
- Empty coffee can
- Newspaper

Assess whether you can do the job with just a dab of paint remover while the hardware remains in place. If it's only a small amount of paint, you probably can. If so, just follow the directions on the paint

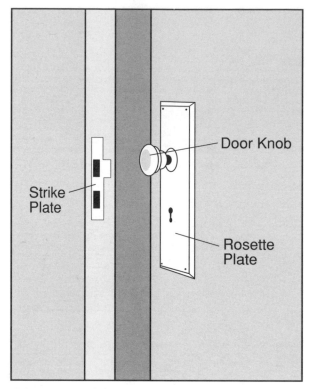

Paint may be dried on your doorknob or rosette plate or even where the door closes onto the strike plate.

Hardware from a door, like this strike plate, can be cleaned quickly with paint stripper.

remover can. Be careful: paint remover is powerful stuff. It sort of makes sense that it will eat away at other surfaces you might splatter or drip it on, like a wood floor or cabinet veneer.

Place a sheet or two of newspaper under the areas where you'll be working. (You may have a dozen little areas set up about the house!) The paint remover won't feel too good on your skin, so wear gloves. Apply the remover where needed at each of your areas, with the pure bristle brush. Wait the suggested amount of time, then walk around with steel wool and wipe it off. You may find that some spots need another coat of remover.

If the fixture was completely painted, it may work better to remove it with the screwdriver and deal with it separately. Sometimes it's easier that

way, at least to avoid getting the paint remover on the door, door jamb, or any other surfaces you don't want to strip.

Submerge the removed hardware, screws and all, in paint remover in a coffee can. If there are several coats of paint on the fixture, or the fixture itself has lots of detail, you may want to let it soak overnight. When you pull it out, use your steel wool to clean the soggy old paint off.

Though most paint removers consist of smelly chemicals, they are, surprisingly, water-soluble. So you can put the fixture in a stainless steel sink or laundry sink and clean/rinse it there (don't put it in a porcelain sink—the paint remover will damage the basin's finish). After towel-drying the fixture, you can buff it with a copper or brass cleaner, depending on the material it is made of.

REPLACING SWITCH AND OUTLET PLATES

These plates are so inexpensive nowadays! Plastic outlet and switch plates come in white, brown, or cream (the three standard colors widely available) and cost between 19 and 50 cents each for a single plate; now, that's cheap! Even if you aren't repainting, changing them is a quick and easy way to clean up a room. New plates in a room look fresh, clean, and, well, new.

There are all kinds of plates out there, by the way. Depending upon how well your hardware store or home center is stocked, you can find plates in brass, wood, and carved metal, in addition to plastic. And you'll find novelty plates, such as ones with Sesame Street characters drawn on them.

I usually just go through the house, apartment, or room and make a list of what plates I need. Rather than writing out the formal type of plate—such as "double switch," "switch and outlet combo," or "cable"—I like to draw a picture of each type of plate needed. Take your illustrated list to the hardware store (you might be a little embarrassed if someone sees it), and buy the plates. Then it's back home for you, the plates, and your screwdriver, and voila!

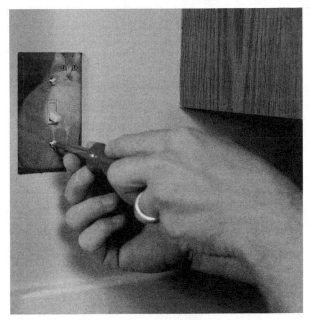

It's easy to replace outlet and switch plates.

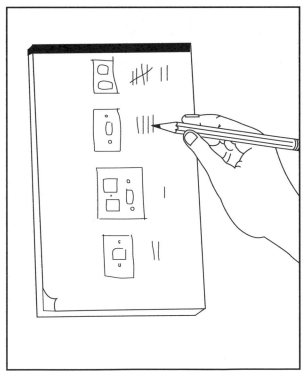

Sketch each plate that you'll want to replace and then go around and tally the number of each needed.

GLOSSARY

ADDITIVES: Thickeners, driers, fungicides, and other chemicals found in a bucket of paint along with its main ingredients of solvent, binder, and pigments.

ALKYD PAINT: What most people think of when they talk about oil-based products; the solvent ingredient is mineral spirits.

BINDER: A component of paint; acrylics are the binder in latex products, oils in alkyd (oil-based) products.

BOLT: Usually refers to double the square footage of a single roll of wallpaper, though triple rolls have been called bolts, too.

BOOKING THE PIECE: The result of folding first one side of a wallpaper strip onto itself (glue side in to the center) and then the other side in similarly, then folding these parts into the center once again; this is done once the glue is applied or activated, before the strip is hung.

BOXING THE PAINT: Refers to intermixing all the gallons of a specific color to ensure an exact color match from gallon to gallon. With custom colors, occasionally one gallon's pigment might be slightly different from another, and that'll show up on the wall.

BRUSHWORK: Using the paintbrush to reach places you can't with a roller, like corners or moldings.

BUTTING THE SEAMS: Aligning the edges of two strips of wallpaper that are hung next to each other so that they touch but don't overlap.

CASING: A molding that circumscribes a window or door.

CAULK: A putty-like product used to fill and seal cracks and crevices.

CAULKING GUN: A device that holds a tube of caulk; enables you to distribute the caulking material by pressing the trigger.

CHISEL: A tool that can be used to shave edges from wood strips; can also be wedged between two pieces of wood for the purpose of prying one free.

DOUBLE-CUTTING: Cutting through two strips of an overlapped wallcovering and then pulling the excess strips off to create a "seamless" seam.

DROP CLOTH, PLASTIC: A thin sheet of plastic (sort of like Saran Wrap, but thicker) used to shield objects and surfaces from paint drips and spray; comes in various thicknesses and sizes.

DROP PATTERN: A repeat on wallpaper that does not line up across the front of the strip; to line up each successive strip, the wallpaper piece must be dropped, usually half the distance of the repeat.

DRUM SANDER: A large floor sander with an internal cylinder that a sheet of sandpaper is wrapped around; it is guided with two hands as you walk erect; and will sand an entire floor surface except the edges.

DRYWALL: A material used in wall construction that consists of gypsum, or plaster, pressed between paper; comes in sheets of various thickness; also called Sheetrock.

DRYWALL TAPE: A strip of paper or nylon mesh that is used to seam gaps between sheets of drywall.

EDGER: The small floor-sanding machine that allows you to sand the edges around a room; uses discs of sandpaper.

EGGSHELL FINISH: A painted surface that has a slight sheen to it; falls between a flat and a satin finish.

FEATHERING: The smooth painted finish that results when you apply paint with a roller and use a light touch just as you lift the roller off the surface.

FLAT FINISH: A painted surface that has no sheen and so does not reflect light; also called matte finish.

GLOSS FINISH: A painted surface that has a good sheen to it and will reflect light well; a bit higher than a semigloss though not as high as a high gloss.

HIGH GLOSS FINISH: A painted surface that has a highly reflective sheen to it; the shiniest you can get.

JOINT COMPOUND: Wet, putty-like material used to repair cracks and seal crevices and gaps between drywall panels; also called drywall compound or plaster.

JOISTS: Big slats of wood that run underneath your floor (and hold everything up).

KEYHOLE SAW: A saw used for cutting drywall; looks like a big steak knife.

LATEX PAINT: A paint product with water as the solvent ingredient.

LEVEL: A framed tool encasing visible vials of water; within each vial is a bubble of air that indicates when the tool is sitting either perfectly level or perfectly plumb (vertical).

MATTE FINISH: See FLAT FINISH.

MINERAL SPIRITS: The oily solvent ingredient found in alkyd (oil-based) paints; also called paint thinner.

NAIL SET: A small metal tool that, when held against the head of a partially driven-in nail and hit with a hammer, will push the nail to just under the surface of the wood (if you hit it right); also called a nail punch.

OUTLET PLATE: The covering over an outlet receptacle that allows you to plug things in without touching any hot wires; usually made of plastic, metal, or wood.

PAINTBRUSH, POLYESTER OR TYNEX: A synthetic-bristle paintbrush made specifically for water-based (latex) products; can also be used for oil-based paints, if specified.

PAINTBRUSH, PURE BRISTLE: A paintbrush made from natural fibers; ideal for oil and alkyd-based products; shouldn't be used with water-based (latex) paints.

PAINT CHIPS: Paint color representations painted on small cards; also called swatches.

PAINT REMOVER: A liquid chemical that, when applied to dried paint, will cause the paint to loosen.

PARQUET FLOORING: A pattern of floorboards resembling a checkerboard, with slats running east-to-west in one square and then north-to-south in the next.

PASTEL: A lighter, paler, version of a color that is created by adding white.

PIGMENTS: The components of paint that give it its color.

PLASTER: See Joint compound.

PLUMB LINE: A perfectly vertical line that is drawn on a wall with a level and is used as a guide for hanging the first strip of wallpaper on each wall.

POLYURETHANE: A finish coating used for sealing and protecting floors and furniture; generally oil-based and containing plastic resins; usually clear with a slight amber tint.

POROUSNESS: The permeability of a surface to fluids; flat finishes are somewhat porous, whereas gloss finishes are not porous at all.

PRE-TRIMMED EDGE: The wallpaper edge that has no selvage (protective excess paper).

PRIMER: The first coat of paint, generally used to seal plaster, wood, metal, or old surfaces and make them ready for the new paint.

PUNCH LIST: Details, usually left to the end of a job, that, when completed, will effectively finish the job.

PUTTY KNIFE: A tool with a 2- to 6-inch-wide blade that's used to smooth plaster onto a wall; looks somewhat like a wide spatula.

RANDOM PATTERN: A wallpaper pattern with no repeat; vertical stripes are a typical random pattern.

RAZOR BLADE, SINGLE EDGE: A small blade used for cutting drywall or trimming wallpaper.

REPEAT: The portion of a wallpaper pattern that repeats itself periodically down the roll.

ROLL OF WALLPAPER: About 36 square feet in America (English rolls are almost half that size); also known as a single roll.

ROLLER HANDLE: A device that's used in conjunction with a paint sleeve to apply paint to a wall.

ROSETTE: The plate attached to a door that the doorknob sticks out of.

SASH: The part of a window that moves and has one or more glass panes; a double-hung window has two sashes.

SATIN FINISH: A painted surface that has a low sheen and so reflects light somewhat; falls between an eggshell (lower sheen) and a semigloss (higher sheen) finish.

SCORE THE WALLS: To make criss-cross cuts through wallpaper onto the wall with a sharp putty knife.

SCRAPER: A tool used to scrape the old floor finish from corners and other spots that a drum sander and edger can't reach.

SCRUBBABLE SURFACE: A surface capable of being wiped down with soap and water without danger of damaging the finish.

SEAM ROLLER: A small tool that is used for rolling the seam down where two edges of wallpaper meet.

SELVAGE: An additional portion of paper on both edges of a roll of wallpaper that protects the roll from damage in shipping; must be cut off before hanging the paper; more common on expensive, hand-printed papers; most wallcoverings come pre-trimmed (no selvage) nowadays.

SEMI-GLOSS FINISH: A painted surface that has a low sheen and reflects light a bit more than a satin finish.

SHEEN: The reflectiveness of a painted surface.

SHEETROCK: See DRYWALL.

SHELLAC: An alchohol-based primer that's usually used for sealing water stains or knots in new wood.

SHINERS: Nail heads seen on the surface of floorboards or even extend out a bit.

SIZE: A clear latex coating that is applied to a wall before wallpaper.

SLEEVE: The fuzzy hollow cylinder that is fitted onto a roller handle and used for rolling paint onto a surface; also known as the roller.

SMOOTHING BRUSH: A comb-shaped brush with short (1-inch) or long (3-inch) bristles that is used to help smooth a wallpaper strip into place on a wall.

SMOOTHING KNIFE: A tool made of flexible plastic that is used to help smooth a wallpaper strip into place on a wall.

SOLVENT: A component of paint that forms the base for the paint solution; in latex products the solvent is water, in alkyd (oil-based) products it's mineral spirits.

SPACKLE: A plasterlike, material that is used to patch holes and cracks on a wall; also called drywall compound.

SPOT-PRIMING: Priming just an area or spot as opposed to an entire wall, ceiling, or door.

STRAIGHT MATCH: A pattern on wallpaper that repeats itself at the same level across the front of the strip, from left to right.

STRIPPABLE VINYL: The easy kind, if you're removing it from the wall; should peel right off in whole sheets when grabbed by the corner.

SUBFLOOR: The layer of floor that sits between the floor joists and the floorboards, usually consists of plywood sheets.

SWATCH: See PAINT CHIPS.

SWITCH PLATE: The covering over an electrical switch that lets you operate the switch without sticking your finger into the connection; usually plastic, metal, or wood.

TAPING KNIFE: Like a putty knife but with a wider blade (10 to 14 inches wide); used for affixing drywall tape to drywall seams; also great as a guide when trimming wallpaper.

TONGUE-AND-GROOVE PLANK: A floor plank that has a valley on one long edge and a bead cut onto the opposite edge; when laid out side-by-side as a floor, tongue-and-groove planks interlock.

TOOTH: To give "tooth" to a surface means to dull it by sanding; usually done to a glossy surface.

TORPEDO LEVEL: A smaller version of a level, usually about six inches long.

TSP: Trisodium phosphate; diluted with water and used to wash down surfaces to ready them for paint.

URETHANE: A water-based finish coating with plastic resins that is used to seal floors and furniture; dries clear and, unlike polyurethane, usually has no amber tint.

WAINSCOTING: The lower segment of a wall usually consisting of a molding, paneling or wallpaper, and base molding.

WALLPAPER

  ANAGLYPTA: Unpainted embossed paper; usually painted once installed.

  FLOCKS: Also called embossed, or raised, paper; usually has a velveteen coating.

  GRASSCLOTH: Thick mesh-woven paper, usually with paper backing; generally without a repeat.

  PREPASTED: Paper with dry adhesive on the back; the glue is activated by dipping the strip in water.

  STANDARD: A wallcovering with paper facing and paper backing.

  VINYL: Rubber coated paper; can have paper, vinyl, or cloth backing.

WALLPAPER REMOVER: A water-soluable liquid that, when applied to wallpaper-covered walls, loosens the wallpaper glue.

WASHABLE SURFACE: A surface capable of being wiped down with a wet sponge without danger of damaging the finish.

WATER TRAY: A container used for dipping dry prepasted strips of wallpaper to activate the glue; measures about 3 feet long by 6 inches deep.

WIRE BRUSH: Looks just like a hairbrush, but the bristles are unflexible wire; used to clean loosened and flaking paint from a paintbrush.

INDEX

Y

NOTES

NOTES